BERNARD NESFIELD-COOKSON has le
a businessman, school teacher, lecturer and v
principal of Hawkwood College, an indepe
cation. He is the author of several books, including *Rudolf Steiner's Vision of Love* and *The Mystery of the Two Jesus Children*.

By the same author:

Rudolf Steiner's Vision of Love
William Blake: Prophet of Universal Brotherhood
Michael and the Two-Horned Beast
Johannes' Pilgrimage in Rudolf Steiner's first Mystery Play
The Mystery of the Two Jesus Children

AT THE DAWN OF A NEW CONSCIOUSNESS

Art, Philosophy and the Birth of the Modern World

Bernard Nesfield-Cookson

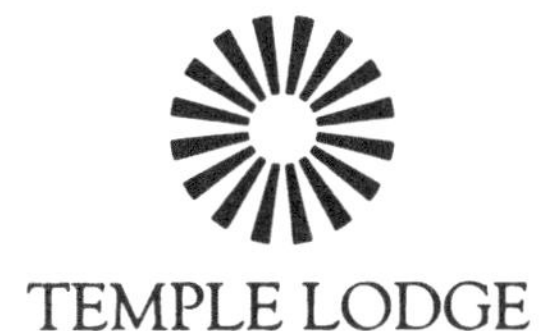

TEMPLE LODGE

Temple Lodge Publishing
Hillside House, The Square
Forest Row, RH18 5ES

www.templelodge.com

Published by Temple Lodge 2010

A catalogue record for this book is available from the British Library

ISBN 978 1 906999 11 7

Cover by Andrew Morgan Design
Typeset by DP Photosetting, Neath, West Glamorgan
Printed and bound by Gutenberg Press Ltd, Malta.

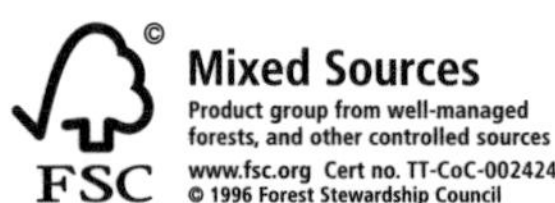

The paper used for this book is FSC-certified and totally chlorine-free. FSC (the Forest Stewardship Council) is an international network to promote responsible management of the world's forests.

For the family and all Florencophiles

Contents

List of Plates

Acknowledgements

I wish to thank Margaret Jonas for her careful copy editing, and Sevak Gulbekian of Temple Lodge Publishing for his interest and willingness to publish this attempt to illustrate a complex theme.

I also wish to put on record my abiding gratitude to my aunt Getrude Sargeant who lived and worked in Italy for many years. From her I imbibed a keen interest in Italian art and a deep love for the spirit of St Francis of Assisi.

Prologue

> The real purpose of history is to explain the present—to show how *we and our ways* came about, and thus partially to interpret us to ourselves.
>
> *(Percy A. Scholes)*[1]

> From primitive times to the present, one may read the condition of the human race in their spiritual, mental and physical attributes through the depiction of art.
>
> *(Emily Palmer Caper)*[2]

> Our attitude to Art largely derives from the Renaissance, more particularly from Florence, where the modern world was born.
>
> *(John Lane)*[3]

The aim of the following pages is to study in some detail aspects of what Rudolf Steiner spoke of as the consciousness soul; in particular in regard to its manifestation in the fifteenth century. For instance, we shall be concerned with the aspect of the consciousness soul, which, inter alia, could be designated 'objective self-consciousness', or, differently expressed, the ability to look at oneself as an object in the same way that we look at, for instance, a table, a plant, or an animal as an object. The endeavour will be made to illustrate this idea, and other aspects of the consciousness soul, by showing how they reflect facts which found expression particularly in fifteenth century Florentine painting, sculpture and architecture, on the one hand, and with the impulses issuing from the Platonic Academy (Accademia Platonica) which was founded by Cosimo de'Medici (1389–1464)—together with, in particular, the young and highly talented Marsilio Ficino (1433–99), round about 1460, and the latter's pupil, Comte Giovanni Pico della Mirandola (1463–94), on the other.

The Italian Renaissance is considered by historians to be the beginning of the modern age. The name itself literally means 'rebirth', an accurate description of this period of innovation in both the sciences and the arts. Renaissance thinkers turned to the texts of the ancient world for refreshed understanding of themselves and the world in which they lived. This living interest in history, literature and the arts was the 'birth' of a whole new way of thinking, one which centred on the world of mankind as much as, if not more than, that of God. This new mode of thinking, called *Humanism*, was in accord with the Greek concept 'man as the measure of all things'.

The Renaissance meant a change in point of view, the emergence of new ideas, and consequently the need of new forms for their expression.

Sculpture began to be conceived 'in the round', instead of as *relief* decorations on cathedrals (Chartres Cathedral, for instance). Mathematical, geometrical perspective and light were also introduced into art, perfecting the sense of three-dimensional reality.

This tendency then appeared in art and, in the fifteenth century, the beginnings of modern science. With the study of the visible, physical world came the birth of the consciousness soul. Men and women became self-conscious in a new way; instead of looking inwards, characteristic of the Middle Ages, they began looking outwards with greater intensity than hitherto, observing in ever greater detail the world around them. The human being, conscious of his or her separate, individual being, observed the phenomena of the world of nature from his or her particular standpoint.

Of course, self-consciousness had prevailed for a long period before the fifteenth century, but, from then on, the self began to be 'looked at' as an *object*; men and women began to look at themselves objectively. We could, therefore, speak of the emergence of objective self-consciousness—hence such fields of study as: the analysis of the human soul (psychoanalysis), human behaviour (psychology and anthropology), and the like.

Bernard Berenson in his essay on Venetian painters of the Renaissance (see bibliography) towards the end of the nineteenth century, remarks that the 1000 years that elapsed since the Roman Emperor Constantine established toleration of Christianity throughout the empire had been not inaptly compared to the first 15 or so years in the life of the individual; these early years, he maintains, were characterized by tutelage and unconsciousness of personality. But about the threshold of the fifteenth century something happened in Europe that happens in the lives of all mature individual human beings—an awakening to the sense of individuality. Although, as Berenson comments, it was experienced to a greater or lesser degree everywhere, it was Italy—which, we would qualify, in particular Florence—felt the awakening earlier than the rest of Europe, and felt it far more strongly. One of the first manifestations of this awakening was 'a boundless and insatiable curiosity, urging people to find out all they could about the world and about man himself'. This 'curiosity' led inevitably to an increased interest in human life and to an acceptance of things for what they were, in short, for their intrinsic quality.

The moment people stopped looking fixedly towards heaven, their eyes fell upon the earth, and they began to see much upon its surface that was pleasant. Their own faces and figures must have struck them as surprisingly interesting and, considering how little St Bernard and other medieval saints—doctors (of the Church)—had led them to expect, singularly beautiful. A new feeling arose that mere living in a physical body, surrounded by a physical world, was to be cherished.

1. The Consciousness Soul

Our study opens with a few statements which are intended to serve as an introductory explanation for those who are not familiar with Rudolf Steiner's spiritual science, of the three sister-concepts in relation to the evolution of the human soul, namely, the sentient soul, the intellectual soul and the already mentioned consciousness soul.

Steiner states that the sentient soul developed in the period in which man[4] in Ancient Egypt and Chaldea acted primarily from motives rising out of the feeling life. The inwardness of the sentient soul manifests itself in medieval Christian art. The powerful stream of Christ-like feeling which went out from St Francis of Assisi 'awakened' painting in Italy during the thirteenth century. Giotto's art becomes the language for those feelings which move human beings' hearts at some event and which bind them together.

Forces of the intellectual soul manifest themselves in the mathematics and geometry of Gothic cathedrals, as practised in the Masons' Guilds; in the same way, these forces built the thought-structures of the scholastic movement. When man reached this stage of his development, the emergence of the intellectual soul, he began to engage reason in regard to his emotions; his feeling life was still rich, but his intellect began the all-significant task of ordering and controlling it. The full greatness of the intellectual soul, or mind soul as it is also called, can be experienced above all through the philosophy of ancient Greece (in particular, Aristotle), or through medieval Christian art and the intellectualism of such a thinker as Thomas Aquinas (1225–74), the Italian scholastic philosopher and theologian.

The development of the third principle, the consciousness soul is, according to Rudolf Steiner, the special task of our era. It embodies a new element which, as indicated already, began to find clear expression in the fifteenth century, particularly in Florence.[5]

A.C. Harwood, in an article entitled 'The Historical Process and the Individual' (in *The Faithful Thinker*, Hodder and Stoughton, 1961) wrote:

> Greek thinking, like all thinking, depends on the activity of the *thinker*, but there was never any doubt in the Greek mind that it was concerned with the *real* world of ideas. The substance of thought—ideas—was far more *real* than the substance of the phenomenal world. [We may think

> of Plato here]. Thinking, alone and unaided, could attain the True, the Beautiful and the Good. This belief in the intrinsic ability of thinking to reach ultimate truth permeated deeply, though with growing doubts, into the Middle Ages. It is partly for this reason that Steiner described the whole of the epoch from the birth of Hellas to the rise of the modern age as that of the Intellectual or Mind Soul.

Harwood continues:

> It is one of the characteristics of the consciousness of the modern age [i.e. since the fifteenth century] that it can take nothing for granted. Everything comes under question. [Increasingly since the dawn of the consciousness soul] the 'given' of tradition has come to an end. Even in science hypothesis has taken the place of knowledge, and the modern scientist has largely abandoned his original search for truth, and is content to discover if it 'works'. At every point the modern consciousness has to strive for the *truth*. But striving in thinking is essentially a spiritual activity . . . It was because he believed that thorough thinking must ultimately penetrate to the spiritual world that Steiner first called the modern soul in English the 'consciousness' soul. Later he preferred to use the term 'spiritual' soul.

It should be mentioned here that in these few pages no more than a few aspects of the consciousness soul can be discussed.

Preparing the ground, as it were, for a more detailed exposition regarding the dawn of our present age being ushered in by fifteenth century Florentine art and philosophy, a passage from Hildegard Gerbert's essay *Education through Art* is quoted here.

> The dawn of the consciousness soul in the Renaissance overpowers the capacity to grasp the world with the forces of feeling. As the physical world with its laws of space gains importance, the inner world of pictures fades away. In place of a composition, which in Giotto still springs into existence like a true imagination out of soul-spiritual depths, the attempt is made to organize the picture according to the laws of perspective, towards a vanishing point which reflects the ego-standpoint of the onlooker. . . . An interest in landscape and in still life comes about simultaneously with the natural sciences. In the North [Dutch and Flemish artists] interior space in which the individuality shuts himself off from the world becomes important.
>
> The consciousness soul, which develops through confrontation with the earthly, must experience within itself the contrast of light and

> darkness, the struggle of good and evil. . . . This struggle penetrates into painting as chiaroscuro . . .[6]

For the sake of further clarification a passage is quoted here from Dietrich Asten's essay *America's Way, The Tasks Ahead*, which characterizes the soul principles as follows:

> A person's inner life consists of three distinct experiences. First of all, he reacts to impressions from the world around him with feelings that cover the whole range from boundless joy to painful emotions. He lives in the *sentient soul.* Out of this sphere thinking gradually arises and leads him to reason about the feelings he experiences. He learns to deal with life rationally. He understands and comprehends. He has reached the stage of the *intellectual soul* [also known as the *mind soul*]. Finally, he acquires, in addition to the wealth of feeling and to the faculty of intellect, the knowledge of self and the consciousness of himself as an individual. This consciousness of self accompanies him when he feels and when he thinks. It is the fulcrum that supports an awareness of his identity. It is the soul in the soul which can be described as the *consciousness soul.*

Margaret Bennell, referring to the time preceding the dawn of the early Renaissance, in particular to the Middle Ages when people looked for guidance in their daily lives to such an authority as the Church, speaks of man as living in the group soul,

> . . . but with his own ego unawakened or still weak, he was helpless before life if detached from that group's encouraging support. Man's new task was to develop the seed of his own egohood, so that, *standing alone in freedom*, he could make free decisions. A thoughtful study of history reveals this gradual change, which even yet is not complete, from men living entirely within the life-stream of their tribe or family, to men beginning to free themselves . . . and to stand alone, supported by their own inner forces in the place of group custom and convention.[7]

As mentioned already, the aim of the present study is to show that it was in particular quattrocento Florentine art (painting, sculpture and architecture) which revealed basic aspects of the early Renaissance worldview that formed the very foundations of the modern era. Consideration will also be given to some aspects of fifteenth century Flemish painting.

The intelligence of Italy—indeed of Western Europe as a whole—had grown tired of and disillusioned with the monastic ideal of life, and the one-sided aim of the scholastic systems to exalt heavenly concerns by ignoring, degrading things terrestrial. The Renaissance sought to give just recognition to man.

It should be mentioned here, in passing, that the presence and activity of the consciousness soul had been foreshadowed in England as early as the thirteenth century by, for instance, the signing of the Magna Carta in 1215 by King John, and the life and work of the philosopher and scientist Roger Bacon (c.1214–1294).[8]

During the fourteenth and fifteenth centuries proto-reformers such as John Wycliffe (c.1320–84) and the Lollards in England who attacked the Church for its worldliness and corruption, and held that the Bible, interpreted by the *individual*, provided the only rule necessary for a holy life. In Bohemia, the religious reformer Jan Hus (c.1372–1415), who was greatly influenced by John Wycliffe, denounced ecclesiastical abuses and challenged the authority of Rome.

What one sees here is the onset of a marked increase in individual freedom and autonomy, features which assumed greater prominence during the fifteenth century in Florence.

2. The Renaissance: Fifteenth Century Florence

The general dates given for the Renaissance are 1400–1550/1600. But it would be justified to suggest that it started much earlier, especially in Italy. The poet and scholar, famous for his sonnets, which quickly influenced poets in many European countries, Francesco Petrarca (Petrarch), the son of an exiled Florentine notary, is sometimes hailed as the first 'modern' man. He died in 1374. It is worth pausing here for a moment to observe an episode which, on the surface, may not appear to be of any relevance to our present considerations.

Sometime in the year 1336 Petrarch did something which no man in history had done before: he climbed a mountain to see the view. Obviously, people before him had climbed mountains, but it was always for some utilitarian reason—in search of food, to escape marauding robbers, to discover fresh grazing land. But no one before Petrarch—at least there is no record of anyone prior to him doing this—had climbed a mountain simply to see the view, for aesthetic reasons. 'Yesterday', Petrarch wrote in a letter to a friend, 'I climbed the highest mountain of our region, motivated solely by the wish to experience its renowned height. For many reasons this has been in my soul.' It is clear from Petrarch's letter that when he finally reached the top of the mountain he underwent a strong emotional and psychic experience. The 'unaccustomed wind' swirled around him; but more than the powerful wind, what clearly overcame him was the hitherto unseen *space* that opened out before him. He was dazzled by the 'wide, freely shifting vistas'. Their wondrous and 'disturbing' expanse shocked the poet and he was, he wrote, 'immediately awestruck'.

In his book *A Secret History of Consciousness*, Gary Lachman, discussing in some detail Petrarch's experience, comments:

> What Petrarch's terrible ascent of Mount Ventoux—in the true, accurate sense of the word 'terrible'—inaugurated was not simply the beginning of ski lodges and vista points in the Rockies and other mountain chains, but a *new, unprecedented appreciation of space* [my emphasis]. . . . Petrarch had taken the first step in a completely new understanding of the world—an understanding that we accept without a moment's thought and take for granted, but that, like so much of our experience, is actually the result of a profound change in human consciousness.

The experience Petrarch wrote about in the letter referred to entailed the metamorphosis of consciousness. He became conscious of a 'new' world; no longer the flat, two-dimensional world of the Middle Ages, but the three-dimensional world of distance, space, 'vanishing points' and receding horizons. In short, the world of *perspective*.[9] In many ways Petrarch was one of the first men of the Renaissance: he translated and collected classical manuscripts, visited Rome for the ruins of antiquity rather than the splendours of the Church, and in his extensive letters and essays on religious, philosophical and political subjects frequently expressed a humanistic point of view.

Among the painters who formed a 'bridge' between the Middle Ages and the early Renaissance just two are mentioned here: the Florentine painter, Cenni di Pepi (Cimabue), 1240–c.1302, and the Florentine painter and architect, Giotto di Bondone. The latter, (1267–1337), is considered the 'Father of the Renaissance'. Characterized as a proto-Renaissance painter, Giotto's work is a transition from the late medieval Byzantine. His innovations were the use of approximate perspective, increased volume of figures, and a depth of emotion which suggests human feeling instead of static and passive icons. Neither of these two artists was a medieval figure in spite of the piety and traditionalism of their subject-matter. What we see happening here is that, as James Laver expresses it:

> Some new wind was filling their sails, some new influence guided their pencils, some new notions stimulated their minds.
>
> The Renaissance has been compared with springtime, a spring bringing light and colour into human life again after the long night. . . . This world became something more than the dark antechamber of a hoped-for heaven, . . . the dry roots put forth new blossoms, and the individual was born . . .[10]

The men and women who lived during the period of the Renaissance must have felt a growing sense of release. Like the Europeans who first reached the Americas in 1492, they sensed that they were entering a new world, a world of wondrous possibilities. It would have been very strange if this new attitude and new experiences had not been reflected in their art and architecture.

As the Renaissance spread so too did the belief that Europeans were creating an entirely new world and culture. Long standing beliefs were tested. The humanistic thinking (see below) prepared the world for the thinkers and scientists of the seventeenth century. The development of modern science was born from the Renaissance idea that humankind rules nature. The concept of human freedom was adopted during the Renaissance.

On a number of occasions Rudolf Steiner specified the year 1413 as being that of the birth of the consciousness soul. However, that this particular date should not be taken too literally is made clear by him in a lecture he gave on 18 October 1918:

> It is impossible to determine the precise moment when an individual arrives at puberty; the onset is gradual and then runs its course to full physical maturity. And the same applies, of course, to the year 1413 which marks the birth of the consciousness soul. The new consciousness develops gradually and does not immediately manifest itself everywhere in full maturity ... When, looking back to the period before the fifteenth century ... we cannot help turning our attention to the ... situation which existed in civilized Europe throughout the whole of the Middle Ages and which was still intimately related to the whole psychic condition of the Greco-Latin epoch. I am referring to the form which Catholicism that was subject to the Papacy had gradually developed over the centuries out of the Roman Empire. We cannot understand Catholicism before the great turning point which marks the birth times unless we bear in mind that it was a universalist impulse and that, as such, it spread far and wide.[11]

In the same lecture Steiner developed this theme somewhat further: The Catholicism which emanated from Rome through centuries Steiner describes as being 'universalist', as being a universal impulse which was the most powerful force animating European civilization. In order to exert and maintain its power the Church counted upon a susceptibility of the human soul to impulsion; in other words, it influenced those who had not yet begun to develop the consciousness soul. Up to the fifteenth century 'intelligence was to some extent instinctive, it had not yet been impregnated with the consciousness soul'. In short, mankind did not yet possess the capacity for completely independent, free, objective reflection. Such reflection, Steiner states, only became possible when man achieved *self dependence* through the consciousness soul.

Jacob Burckhardt in *The Civilization of the Renaissance in Italy*, discussing the development of the individual, makes the following observation which is of interest here:

> In the Middle Ages both sides of human consciousness—that which was turned within as that which was turned without—lay dreaming or half awake beneath a common veil. The veil was woven of faith, illusion, and childish prepossession, through which the world and history were seen clad in strange hues. Man was conscious of himself only as a member of a race, people, party, family, or corporation—only through some general category.[12]

Burckhardt gives expression here to what Rudolf Steiner designates as the *group soul.* Members of a group soul do not, of course, experience themselves as separate individuals; each member does not seek to have a 'space' to him- or herself.[13]

As already indicated, signs that a change in consciousness was going to come about made their preliminary appearance in art in the work of the Florentine painter Giotto di Bondone (c.1267–1337) who, as just mentioned formed a bridge, as it were, between the Middle Ages and the Renaissance.

Burckhardt goes on to say:

> In Italy an objective treatment . . . of all the things of this world became possible. The subjective side at the same time asserted itself with corresponding emphasis, man became a spiritual *individual. And recognized himself as such* [my emphases].

Burckhardt then makes a somewhat sweeping observation in the first sentence which follows:

> Dante's great poem would have been impossible in any other country of Europe, if only for the reason that all still lay under the spell of race. For Italy the august poet, through the wealth of individuality which he set forth, was the most national herald of his time.

In *Purgatorio* (Canto 11:94–6) Dante Alighieri (1265–1321), who was Giotto's contemporary, commenting on the fleeting nature of artistic reputation, notes that:

> Cimabue once thought that he held the field in painting, and Giotto has the praise, so much so that the other's fame is obscured.

Why did Giotto so quickly surpass his teacher? Art historians have noted that while Cimabue began to break away from the Byzantine style of painting that had dominated Europe since the beginning of the Middle

Ages, Giotto's innovations were much more radical and systematic. His tentative use of perspective and his portrayal of figures as individuals, each with a distinctive personality, resulted in a realism that would have appealed to the fourteenth century Florentine middle class. When the era of the consciousness soul opened in the early fifteenth century, a growing number of people desired to take their affairs into their own hands. They wanted to discuss issues which affected them; they were no longer willing to allow others to decide things for them.[14] An example illustrating the impulse of the consciousness soul is that of the attitude of Jan Hus (c.1372–1415) mentioned briefly already. In 1408 he defied a Papal Bull which alleged heretical teaching by continuing to preach and was excommunicated in 1411. After writing his main work, *De Ecclesia (*1413, *On the Church*) he was called before a general council at Constance, but he refused to recant and was burnt at the stake.[15]

This is a clear example of the consciousness soul rising in protest against the petrified forms inherited from the era of the intellectual soul. In medieval times religion had become petrified in outer form. What in earlier times had been spiritual revelation had become dogma. One could go so far as to say, with justification, that the Church usurped spiritual life, preaching its own omniscience and demanding blind faith on the part of its adherents.

The epoch of the consciousness soul 'demands that man should stand on his own two feet, be self-sufficient whenever required and, as personality, emancipate himself'.[16] He should no longer allow himself to be persuaded as to what he should believe. He must work out his own religious belief for himself. Only a genuine concern for each other can bring into being a truly human community. Now, a characteristic feature of the epoch of the consciousness soul is man's isolation. He is inwardly isolated from his neighbour, an inevitable consequence of individuality, of the development of personality. But this separative tendency must be counterbalanced by the cultivation of an active concern of every person for his or her neighbour. The following verse, spoken by Rudolf Steiner in a lecture he gave in Berlin on 1 September 1914, that is, a few weeks after the outbreak of the First World War, may give us some idea of what is meant here by the 'cultivation of a genuine and active concern':

Whilst pain is felt by you alone
And not by me,
Christ goes unrecognized

To do his work within the world.
For the spirit cannot grow strong
If it has the power only to feel
The suffering your own body undergoes.[17]

When the consciousness soul was free to begin its full development in European nations in the fifteenth century[18] man began, for the first time in history, to become fully conscious of his spiritual being, of his ego; he experienced the faculty of thinking as his own individual activity, that is, no longer imposed upon him. Moreover, he began to permeate his life of feeling with thought, so that, for instance, he could begin to control his passions naturally from 'within', no longer so dependent on support from external laws and conventions. He also became able to look at himself objectively in his relationship to his fellow men. This signified considerable advance in the moral sphere, 'since', as Faulkner Jones expresses it, 'all truly moral actions must arise from a recognition of the relation of man to man'.[19]

Closely connected with man's increasing focus on, attention to, the sense perceptible material world—Italian Renaissance artists were among the first to paint secular scenes, breaking away from the purely religious art of medieval painters—and his development of the individual reason, is the growth of the world outlook known as materialism, which denies the possibility of man's gaining direct knowledge of any 'world' other than that vouchsafed to his sense organs.

The consciousness soul finds expression in and through the physical body. We could say that man, with the birth of the consciousness soul has completely descended into his physical body and stands with his feet firmly planted on the earth. As a consequence of this firm contact with the physical earth, man became increasingly conscious, aware of all that surrounds him on the material plane. This awareness forms the foundation on which the consciousness soul culture is based. Its clearest manifestation is the rapid development—in the last few centuries—of the natural sciences; out of which grew the industrial civilization. Dietrich V. Asten, in the essay mentioned earlier, observes that a modern American gains consciousness of self and of the world around him primarily through his contact with the material world. Matter, Asten claims, is the starting point for the American's physical and spiritual endeavours. He quotes the following lines from a passage in an article, 'First Glimpses of a New World' which Robert Hutchins wrote for the *Saturday Review* in 1965; '[The American] is not at home with anything he cannot count, because he is not sure of any other measure. He cannot estimate or appraise quality. This leaves him with quantity.'[20]

Human beings of the consciousness soul period need to strive to acquire the ability to perceive the spiritual worlds (as, for instance, the clairvoyant Ancient Egyptian priests still perceived them without having made any conscious effort to do so), but this cannot be done without self-development, which, inter alia, includes complete selflessness. If this is achieved then, said Steiner, just as the external world of matter reveals itself to the physical senses, the spiritual world 'lying behind' the external world reveals itself to the spiritual senses.

In connection with the theme of complete selflessness it is rewarding to look at Shakespeare's play *King Lear,* in particular at the king's youngest daughter, Cordelia. In a book entitled *The Other World of Myths and Fairy Tales* which deserves to be better known than has hitherto been the case, Madge Childs devotes the last chapter to a study of Shakespeare's *King Lear.* Now, we learn from Rudolf Steiner that it is Britain's mission in world evolution to develop the consciousness soul. Thus, Childs writes, 'it was fitting for King Lear and his daughter Cordelia to be British; as it was for Shakespeare himself, the earliest portrayer of the consciousness soul in drama. Cordelia is representative of the heart forces (her very name speaks of this quality): of unselfish love, truth and courage. It is through the forces of the heart that one is enabled to attain knowledge of the spiritual world. It is the courage to go beyond the traditional and conventional in one's thinking. And finally', Childs states, 'it is the courage, in full awareness and ego control, to cross the threshold of our own subconscious. Here we will meet and must overcome the impulses of evil . . .'[21]

As has been stressed already, the fifteenth century ushered in an era in the western hemisphere in which the human individuality began to develop more and more in full objective I-consciousness. Steiner stresses that it is precisely because of the separateness that we see in the individual today when the individuality is developing, when I-consciousness is developing fully, when the consciousness soul is, as it were, becoming integrated in itself, that a social life comes into being which is imbued through and through with the moral quality which may be characterized by the realization that the well-being of the individual will depend entirely upon the well-being of the whole.[22]

In the same lecture cycle in which Steiner makes this point[23] he also states that in the era of the consciousness soul complete freedom of thought in the sphere of religion should come into being. What religious convictions an individual holds should rest wholly within the power of his or her individuality. Complete freedom of thought in the domain of religion is a fundamental right of every individual.

During the 14 centuries or so after the death and Resurrection of Christ, man's relationship to Him was essentially that of believing in Him, endeavouring to be like Him, loving Him. We could think here of St Francis of Assisi among numerous other devout Christians. But there was, as yet, no apparent need to understand Him. This need came into being with the beginning of the age of the consciousness soul at a time when man began to think more than earlier, independently of higher ecclesiastical authority.

The Middle Ages represent the last glimmer of the ancient clairvoyance. The conception of the world set forth in Dante Alighieri's (1265–1321) *Commedia*[24] is medieval. The particular features of it are Dante's own invention. Dante is not able to see by actual clairvoyance into the realm of the supersensible. He can, in short, no longer *experience* it; but, in keeping with the time in which he lived, he could still *feel* it. In Dante the age-old 'religiousness' still speaks. Arnold Freeman spoke of Dante in the following vein:

> He represents the deathbed phase of man's dependence upon the Divine Spiritual. His real guide through *Inferno* and *Purgatorio* was not Virgil but Moses. According to quasi-divine moral law—authority given from above; to human beings not yet evolved to self-dependence—Dante pronounces the awe-inspiring theological-ethical verdicts upon great and small, upon contemporaries and predecessors. Those who take their moral standards from any kind of 'authority'; those who turn to church or scripture, state or society, for moral guidance; those who live by tradition or rule or routine; all such persons are living in the wake of Dante.[25]

As a result of losing the 'divine guidance' men and women are enabled to evolve into self-consciousness and self-dependence, into moral responsibility and selfhood and freedom.

It has been mentioned already that the consciousness soul is characterized especially by objectivity, which results from the ability of the self to withdraw from the object being observed. In this regard, as indicated above, we could speak of *objective self-consciousness*. Whereas people of, say, early medieval times felt themselves to be integrally linked with the world around them, we now—particularly since the fifteenth century—see the world, including our fellow human beings, as totally separate from us. It was first from the beginning of the fifteenth century that men and women in general began to experience themselves as 'I', that is, as individualities separated from other individualities. (As already indicated modern men and women, compared with, say, 500–600 years ago, can view *themselves* objectively. Hence such fields of study as psychoanalysis, psychology and anthropology). From the eighth century BC to, say, the early part of the fifteenth century AD this was not such a general experience:

> The human being has grown out of the group soul condition and emancipates himself from it increasingly.... The human beings of earlier times were born into connections, into the tribe, the race. Later we shall live in the connections and associations which people create for themselves, uniting in groups with those of similar ideas while retaining their complete freedom and individuality.[26]

As stated already, in these pages we are largely concerned with the 'birth' of the consciousness soul as it manifested itself in Florence in the fifteenth century; some attention will also be paid to Central Europe, to Flanders and Germany. However, in an endeavour to clarify how Steiner envisaged the change in the soul-constitution of man by the withdrawal from the group-soul, it seems justified here to digress a little.

According to Rudolf Steiner the consciousness soul (spectator consciousness) is particularly fully developed in the English people. On one occasion, discussing the change just mentioned, Rudolf Steiner illustrated it by contrasting Hector, the leader of the Trojan forces in the Trojan War in Homer's *Iliad*, with Shakespeare's Hamlet. The former was a strong, vigorous and co-ordinated personality, supported by being embedded in devotion to his family and to his city, Troy; the latter, Hamlet, thrown off his balance by being stripped, by circumstances, of the support of family and 'group' and compelled to stand alone when his ego is not yet sufficiently mature for such a test, so that he becomes a waverer, a ditherer.

Shakespeare, in *Hamlet*, shows us how the new born ego-consciousness is isolated on three levels—it is cut off from the surrounding world, from unreflective action, and from the earlier interweaving with fellow human beings. On all three levels it looks on from without. Here we see something entirely new in man's 'soul-history'—the spectator consciousness, the onlooker.

A significant feature of the whole play, *Hamlet*, is that it is full of images of death and dying; a cavalcade of death which leads to the moving picture of Hamlet standing in the grave with Yorick's skull in his hand.[27] The forces of ego-consciousness are most strikingly revealed in Hamlet's soliloquies. These discourses with himself express 'the consciousness philosophizing with itself, the ego-forces of the consciousness soul'.[28]

Later, when we come to consider Renaissance works of art we shall meet paintings which portray Death approaching both young and old. These appear about 200 years after the deadly plague, probably bubonic, which was widespread in Asia and Europe in the fourteenth century. Rudolf Steiner spoke on a number of occasions of the intimate relationship prevailing between the consciousness soul and the experience of death.[29] Owen Barfield, in his intriguing book *Romanticism comes of Age* states:

> Of the many startling and obvious truths to which Steiner was nevertheless alone in drawing attention, there is none more paramount to the whole of human experience than the truth that consciousness, based as it is on a perpetual wastage of the nervous and sensory tissues, is a direct concomitant of—death. Steiner, beginning his investigations before psychoanalysis was heard of, had set in a beautifully clear light ... the truth that—reflected physically in the cerebro-spinal system and the metabolism—consciousness and life stand at dead opposite poles.

A.C. Harwood takes up this theme in his seminal work *Shakespeare's Prophetic Mind*:

> There is a ... polarity between the system of brain and nerves and that of limbs and metabolism; in the latter the force of life predominates and in the former a perpetual death process. For the brain and nerve system in man consists of substance which is perpetually dying.
>
> It is precisely because there are no life forces at work that consciousness in thinking can become so clear and acute, but is also so withdrawn from actual experience of the living world. This withdrawn consciousness is the spectator consciousness of which we have so clear a picture in *Hamlet*. The play is a 'meditation on death' for no other reason than that it is a picture of the consciousness that uses the forces of death in man.[30]

Margaret Bennell in her book *Shakespeare's Flowering of the Spirit* sums up the points being made here in the words: 'We see Hamlet bearing the birth-pangs of the ego and the changeover from the participating consciousness to the separative consciousness ...'[31]

Alice Turner draws our attention to the fact that, by the fifteenth century, the figure of Death, personified as an animate corpse or skeleton was ubiquitous in European art. The first precursor appears towards the beginning of the fourteenth century with the *Legend of the Three Living and Three Dead*. In it three foppishly dressed youths, or sometimes kings, encounter three desiccated corpses. 'As you are, so once were we', they intone. 'As we are, so will you be.' An unusual mid-fifteenth century painting by Jan van Eyck, *Last Judgement* shows the perfect graphic bridge between the two concepts: the old hell is topped by the new skeletal and grinning Death.

It has been indicated already that an outstanding feature of the period beginning in the fifteenth century was that of freedom and autonomy, emancipation from authority of any kind in the search for individual freedom. This, of course, found expression on a major scale with the onset of the Reformation—in which Martin Luther (1483–1546) played a major role (see above re Hus, Lollards etc.) and the demand for freedom of belief. In the fifteenth century men and women began in earnest to question everything. Johannes Gutenberg's invention of printing from movable type in 1440 changed the tenor of life and it reflected not only the need of the individual to know more, but also the efforts of enquiring minds. The first block-printed Bible, The *Biblia Pauperum* was published in 1455. By 1499 printing had become established in more than 2,500 cities around Europe. By then an estimated 15 million copies had been press printed, representing 30 thousand books. The invention of printing, which brought with it the possibility of increasing numbers of people gaining knowledge in spheres up to then unavailable to them, clearly had a profound effect on their lives, in particular on that of women. Gaia Servadio, in her recent book *Renaissance Woman*, speaks in some detail about this. One of her statements runs: 'Women began to make intellectual efforts. Communication was all-important to that new spirit, and only by learning did women stand a chance of becoming individuals—*individuality being a prime concept of the Italian Renaissance*.'[32]

When, before the advent of the printed book, all books had to be written out by hand and copied, most education was imparted by word of mouth, and there was a natural inclination to accept, on the basis of authority, what a speaker said. Thus when printing made books accessible to the multitude one could read for oneself and still feel quite free, accepting or rejecting the authority of the writer in accordance with his or her judgement.

The artist, Gladys Mayer, in her fascinating essay *Sleeping and Waking and the Life of Art*, wrote of the craftsmen and artists of the Middle Ages as being imbued with veneration for the tasks they undertook. The qualities of love and piety permeate the art proceeding from these times. We can experience the reality of Mayer's statement when we immerse ourselves in the work of Fra Angelico (c.1400–1455) whose frescoes, in the convent of San Marco in Florence, for example, form a 'bridge', as it were, between the fading age of the mind soul, the intellectual soul, and the dawning consciousness soul. Fra Angelico was one of those who still 'flowed' in the stream issuing from his fellow countryman, St Francis of Assisi (c.1181–1226). Michelangelo, commenting on the paintings of Fra Angelico, stated: 'This good man painted with his heart, so that he was able with his pencil to give outward expression to his inner devotion and piety, which I can never achieve, since I do not feel myself to have so well disposed a heart.'[33]

The most obvious changes during Renaissance times are to be found in the paintings and sculpture. Though artists continued the medieval tradition of using religious subjects, illustrating, in particular, stories from the Bible, they combined this with classical ideals of the human figure and an increased interest in depicting nature. To the contemplative, inward-turned gaze of the religious soul-life of the Middle Ages, the outer, visible world was a mystery. From the thirteenth century onwards, however, the human being began to direct his gaze in ever increasing measure outwards into the physical world and to regard it not as something which spoke of varying degrees of darkness and evil, but of love and beauty. In a course of lectures Rudolf Steiner gave in 1916 and 1917 on the *History of Art*[34] Rudolf Steiner described this 'path' of the human soul and spirit as it is mirrored in art, as the creative artist turned from 'absorption in inner clairvoyant vision, or whatever was handed down traditionally as a result of this, to a kind of "falling in love" with the outer world'.[35]

It is true to say that in recent times art hardly enters consciously into the life of most people. It was certainly different in the past when the arts were closely bound up with the religious life. Art was treated with awe and reverence by young and old, rich and poor. The craftsmen and artists of the Middle Ages likewise carried out their tasks with the qualities of veneration, love and piety. It is true, of course, that such qualities were still to be found in artists in the fifteenth century. Fra Angelico was a shining example in this respect. The supreme tenderness and purity of the blues in his paintings give us a picture of profound purity and piety in the soul-life of the artist.[36] But, with the growth of individual self-consciousness which came into being with pronounced power from the fifteenth century onwards, with greater appraisal of values and increasingly conscious of the forces and forms existing in the physical world of nature, we can recognize that spiritual imaginations no longer formed the main 'nourishment' and concern of the artist who became more concerned with the revelations, wonders and beauties of the world of nature than with intimations of a world 'behind' and 'beyond' the visible. The physical world has provided us with a basis for forming the individual ego-consciousness just mentioned. To paraphrase Gottfried Richter (see p. 37), if any abnormal or pathological state of consciousness threatens us with loss of the sense of self we inevitably cling to our sense-perceptions of the world of nature around us in order to restore us to ourselves.

Before proceeding further a few words are in place here as to the meaning of the term Renaissance as it is used in these pages. In the narrower sense, the Renaissance may be confined to the recovery of the culture of Greece and Rome and the revival of belles-lettres and art. After having been warned by the Church for centuries to steer clear of the literature of classic antiquity because, it was maintained, it was full of snares and dangers for a Christian people, the time came—beginning with Petrarch (1304–74), Dante (1265–1321) and Giovanni Boccaccio (1313–75)—when the same people 'opened their eyes and ears' and took both delight and deep interest in the discovery of ancient authors and history.[37] It was indeed an intellectual and artistic new birth that burst forth in Italy, in particular in fifteenth century Florence, a regeneration. But it was more than this. It was a revolt against monastic asceticism and scholasticism, the systems which hindered the free flow of creative activity and intellectual inquiry.

Closely connected with man's physical relationship to the material plane, on the one hand, and the development of his individual reason, on the other, is the growth of a materialistic conception of the world and of man's place in it. We saw earlier that, according to Dietrich V. Asten, today's American gains consciousness of self and of the world around him primarily through his contact with the material world: that matter is the starting point for the American's physical and spiritual endeavours. Such a conception, if not balanced by the realization that the physical object would not exist unless an 'idea', the spiritual, had given birth to it, ultimately denies the possibility of man's being able to gain any knowledge of any sphere other than that accessible to his physical senses.[38] Herein lies one of the challenges issued by the consciousness soul. Another 'danger' inherent in the development of the consciousness soul is that modern man, relying on and proud of his recently gained intellectual faculties and knowledge of the physical world, and, in particular, his self-centred concern about his particular role and place in that world, tends to indulge in a greater or lesser degree of egoism.[39] During the period of the development of the wide-awake consciousness of the scientist who looks upon the external world as a spectator,[40] penetrating the world around him with his intelligence, man, Rudolf Steiner states, also needs to strive to develop another kind of knowledge of it through which he would come to recognize the spiritual element that underlies the world of matter.

Consciousness is 'related' to death, unconsciousness to life. In the death sphere of consciousness the ego becomes conscious of itself. It gets to know itself by making itself the object of observation. We can, therefore, say that man owes his ego-consciousness to death, the forces of death.[41] Another more purely visual theme was that of the Dance of Death. Holbein's sixteenth century interpretation, based on earlier models, is probably best known to many people. The move toward the personification of Death in the fourteenth and fifteenth centuries is echoed in hundreds of pictures and carvings, and can also be found in poetry as well as in the moralities.

Whether or not this move was a response to the deadly plague (Black Death)[42] which was widespread in Asia and Europe in the fourteenth century is moot. What is significant, as Alice Turner points out, is that the art and poetry indicate that soon after the point at which the Catholic Church adopted the doctrine of Purgatory at the Council of Basel-Ferrara-Florence, 1431–1445, hell began to lose its grip on the imagination. Fear of death began to replace the fear of hell.[43]

The break with authority, with ruling traditions and orthodoxies and the ever-repeated demands for freedom, emancipation, self-determination may be regarded as being the most significant feature of the consciousness soul age hitherto. However, as Francis Edmunds suggests, these qualities 'may have been misrepresented at times, freedom and emancipation take supremacy over all other calls and demands in this consciousness age since the fifteenth century'. Edmunds then goes on to point out that '[freedom] in the past meant freedom from outer bondage and compulsion. Today it has acquired a further meaning: a finding of oneself, a birth from within'.[44] In general terms it is justified to say that prior to the beginning of the fifteenth century, obedience, whether to Church or State, had been the prevailing rule. To question the powers divine was sacrilege, to question the governing body, a form of treason.

Incidentally, rather humorously Rudolf Steiner described the turning towards materialism as embodied in the person of St Francis of Assisi whom he called, paradoxically, 'the first great materialist', for he was the first among the religion men of his time who, instead of turning away from the physical world, the world of nature, to seek the spirit, turned to that world with an ardent love for all creation.[45] The spirit of St Francis inspired the painter Giotto in the same direction. Painting began to leave the laws of the two-dimensional world, the non-physical world, and 'enter' into, portray the physical, three-dimensional world.[46] As we shall be considering in due course, early in the age of the consciousness soul, 'linear perspective' was invented[47] and used by numerous painters and sculptors in the Renaissance and since. This was a typical aspect of modern consciousness that endeavoured to paint, sculpture objects exactly as the physical human eye perceives them. With the growth of individual consciousness, intellectual appraising of values in the outer world of nature, art loosened itself from its connection with spiritual insight and imagination and became increasingly concerned with the revelations and beauties of the world of nature. Here we need to be clear in our minds that intellectual 'head' knowledge is really unable to understand the living, that which is creative. It can understand that which has 'become', but not that which is 'becoming'. 'Head' intellect, as distinct from the intellect of the heart,[48] treats the whole that appears in nature as though it were composed of a multitude of tiny parts, ignoring the reality that a whole is qualitatively different from the sum of its parts. Nor can the generally accepted scientific mentality arrive at anything that could be called 'scientific morality'.

Florence was, after Venice, the wealthiest Italian city and Cosimo de'Medici (1389–1464), her first citizen, perhaps the wealthiest man in Europe. Cosimo's love of knowledge was boundless. It is said that he employed 45 scribes who were constantly engaged in the task of copying numerous Greek and Latin authors, on parchment, with beautifully painted initials.[49] Up to the fourteenth century Greek authors were only known through the few Latin translations. It was a historical event which greatly contributed to the absorption of Greek culture in Florence: the Church Council, first held at Ferrara, was transferred to Florence in January 1439, when the plague broke out in Ferrara. This Council was the initiative of John VIII Palaeologus (1392–1448),[50] and Pope Eugenius IV (1383–1447),[51] who wished to unite the Eastern and Roman Churches. Cosimo de'Medici offered hospitality to both the Emperor and the Pope. Meetings took place near Careggi in one of Cosimo's villas. There thinkers and artists strove to connect the profoundest truths of Christianity with ancient philosophies. At the centre of their investigations stood the human being, stood man. He was prized higher than nature. This, perhaps, partly explains why the Florentine Platonic Academy did not penetrate into Aristotle's philosophy of nature with the vigour they applied to Neoplatonism. This does not mean that the Neoplatonists had no interest in the natural, physical world. Far from it, as we shall see. The first documented proof for the existence of the Academy at Careggi was a letter of 1462 addressed to Cosimo de'Medici in which Marsilio Ficino thanks him 'for the Academy at Careggi, the gift you bestowed upon us'. Four years later, at the young age of 35, Ficino became the leader of the academy. Every now and again in Ficino's written works we come across the indication that some of the writings of the Academy could only be read by those who had undergone the necessary preparation.

Rudolf Steiner once spoke of the Florentine Academy and mentioned that one became a member not by knowledge alone, but by proving that one had passed through such supersensible experiences which showed that the spiritual world was a reality, more than a mere concept.[52] Closely associated with the Platonic Academy was the young Count Pico della Mirandola (1463–94). He, in common with Ficino, saw in Christianity the fulfilment of the ancient Mysteries, which from Plato went back to Pythagoras and to Orpheus.

In Florence the fresh interest in the physical world was accompanied and strengthened by the Platonic view that God is not transcendent and aloof, but present in the world in which man lives. Nature offers an explanation of God and therefore the study of nature is morally to be encouraged. Ficino and his circle believed that nature as an instrument of the divine provided a 'stairway to God'. Plato was also embraced because he taught that the study of nature promoted harmony. So, for their picture of the physical world the Florentines of the fifteenth century turned to Plato. The Greek philosopher who, they had found, provided a reasoned foundation for Christian beliefs was also found to provide an equally satisfactory interpretation of the physical universe. Indeed, we should remember that far from being devoted one-sidedly to secular values, the Florentine Renaissance was still an intensely Christian society. Plato insists on the beauty of the universe and he defines beauty in terms of mathematics. Here Plato follows Pythagoras. Plato made mathematics the key to an understanding of the universe. We may remind ourselves here that over the door to his Academy in Athens Plato had the following sentence inscribed, 'Let no man enter who knows no geometry'.

The founding of the Platonic Academy in the early sixties of the fifteenth century by Cosimo de'Medici brought with it a shift from political and social concerns to an intense interest in and speculation about the nature of humankind and the cosmos. Mention has been made already that a number of learned Greeks came to Italy for the Council of Ferrara-Florence during the 1430s. The most important consequence for Florence was the introduction of Platonism by some of the Greeks present and the subsequent development of a Platonic Academy in Florence. Summarizing we could say: in the Renaissance sense Humanism was consistent with religious belief. Humanists believed that the Greek and Roman classics contained the lessons men and women needed to live a moral and effective life. The philosophy of the Renaissance humanists embraced such concepts that God had 'put' us here on earth to have confidence in the achievements of humankind; that man should live in harmony with nature; and that the dignity of man should be recognized and emphasized, rather than the medieval ideal of a life of penance that focused on the hereafter.[53]

The impulses of Florentine Neoplatonism and Humanism, led by Marsilio Ficino and Pico della Mirandola, and 'mentored' by Cosimo de' Medici, radiated out from the Florentine Academy throughout Italy and into Europe. Among the first Englishmen to visit Italy and to come under the influence of Florentine Humanism was William Grocyn (1446?–1519). He studied Greek and Platonic philosophy under Demetrius Chalcondyles (1424–1511), who had been called to Florence by Lorenzo de'Medici in 1479, and Angelo Poliziano (1454–94), poet, philologist and humanist, who was both a friend and protégé of Lorenzo de'Medici, and one of the foremost classical scholars of the Renaissance. After his return from Italy, where he had visited Florence, Rome and Padua, Grocyn had the post of lecturer in Exeter College, University of Oxford, where he found an opportunity of indoctrinating his young countrymen in the new Greek learning.

One of Grocyn's contemporaries was Thomas Linacre (c.1460–1524), an Oxford professor, and the personal physician to both King Henry VII and his son, Henry VIII. Linacre visited Italy in the 1480s, where he became a pupil of Angelo Poliziano. After reading the New Testament in Greek and comparing it with the Latin Vulgate, he wrote in his diary: 'Either this [the original Greek] is not the Gospel ... or we are not Christians'. Yet the Church of Rome still threatened to have anyone killed who read the Scripture in any language other than Latin—though Latin was not the original language of the New Testament.

On his return to Oxford, full of the learning and imbued with the spirit of the Florentine Renaissance, Linacre formed a circle of brilliant Oxford scholars which included William Grocyn and John Colet (1467?–1519). Among his pupils was Desiderius Erasmus (c.1469–1536), the Dutch humanist and scholar.[54] The Renaissance Christian humanists were a varied lot. Italian humanists lived in an entirely different atmosphere from their peers in Germany, France or England. Italian Humanism was literary, artistic, and philosophical, whereas northern Humanism was more overtly religious, even theological. This northern Christian Humanism was best represented by Desiderius Erasmus. At Oxford, Sir Thomas More (1478–1535), Renaissance author and Catholic martyr, had Colet for his confessor and Linacre for his tutor. When he was 17, the death occurred in Italy of a man with whom he was very closely connected though he had never met him in the flesh, Pico della Mirandola. On one occasion Rudolf Steiner spoke of Thomas More as being a 'most significant and gifted pupil of Pico della Mirandola'.[55] There were two major philosophers of the Renaissance whose lives and work impinged upon Elizabethan England: one was the English alchemist, geographer and mathematician, John Dee (1527–1608),[56] and the other was the Italian hermetic thinker, Giordano Bruno (1548–1600). Both were 'occult' philosophers, and both admired and were influenced by Marsilio Ficino and Pico della Mirandola.[57] The poet Edmund Spenser (c.1552–1599) was one of several English poets who was influenced by Marsilio Ficino and Giovanni Pico della Mirandola and their exposition of Platonic theology and Plato's philosophical mythology. They believed not only that all myths hide a profound meaning but also that this ancient pagan mythology is really in agreement with Christianity. 'So', as C. S. Lewis states, 'it is hardly an exaggeration to speak of a tradition of philosophical iconography'.[58]

The aim to combine Christianity with philosophy is also typical of the group known as the Cambridge Platonists (second half of the seventeenth century, including Ralph Cudworth and Henry More). Jill Line has made a detailed study of the influence of the Christian-Platonic philosophy of love in which, she maintains, all Shakespeare's plays and poems have their genesis. The philosopher of this tradition whose ideas Shakespeare most clearly reflects was the scholar-priest Marsilio Ficino.[59] Frances A. Yates gives us a clear picture of the influence the Neoplatonism represented by Ficino and Pico had on the French Academies in her detailed study entitled *The French Academies of the Sixteenth Century.*[60] At the beginning of this study she states that 'one must ... begin with the original Platonic Academy of Florence, for the ideas disseminated there form the background of our subject.' The creative artists searched for ways in which to express the freedom they were gaining. What we could call 'Franciscan Humanism' provided one such way in its newly-revived sense of enjoyment of nature and natural beauty; so different from the denial of the world fostered by the medieval Church's asceticism.[61] The influence of the 'Franciscan movement' can be seen as early as the Giotto frescoes in the church of St Francis at Assisi. But this 'movement' did not indulge in much philosophizing over nature, and the emerging Renaissance culture demanded a more objective appreciation of the world. This, as has already been indicated, was found in the revival of interest in the culture of the ancient world.

Typical of the early Renaissance humanist was Leon Battista Alberti (1404–72). His attitude to the wisdom of the ancients, and to the combining of it with Christianity, was primarily pragmatic and rationalistic—his humanistic religion rejected most of the mystical overtones of contemporary Christianity. Where Alberti is the direct forerunner of later Renaissance Humanism is in his ideas on beauty, drawn from Plato's classical theories on love, beauty and the nature of the universe. He maintained that beauty has objective reality, and is not dependent on mere subjective opinion. An example of the difference appears in the interpretation of Plato's theories on love. Where Alberti considered love primarily in relation to its social function, the Neoplatonists regarded it to be the contemplation of divine beauty. In one of his papers he read before the Middle Atlantic Renaissance Conference in Philadelphia on 29 October 1960, Paul Oskar Kristeller stated that Leon Battista Alberti, philosopher, architect, musician, painter and sculptor, in agreement with Pico della Mirandola, wrote 'Men are themselves the source of their own fortune and misfortune'.[62] In one of Pico della Mirandola's inspired passages God addresses man with the stirring phrase: 'Masterful moulder and sculptor of yourself'.[63]

There is a study of Vitruvian Man illustrating human proportions in one of Leonardo da Vinci's notebooks to which we shall return in a later chapter. In Renaissance terms it expresses much of what Pico della Mirandola argues concerning the capability of humanity to encompass the whole of creation. In what we may term Renaissance mathematics and in Neoplatonism, the square in geometry represents the terrestrial world, the circle the celestial world, and the triangle the divine world. The circle and square in Leonardo da Vinci's drawing represents more than the mathematics of drawing a human being. They represent how the human being encompasses in his reach the whole of the terrestrial and celestial worlds. This image exemplifies the blend of art and science during the Renaissance and provides a perfect example of Leonardo's keen interest in proportion. It also represents a cornerstone of his attempts to relate man to nature. *Encyclopaedia Britannica online* states: 'Leonardo envisaged the great picture chart of the human body he had produced through his anatomical drawings and Vitruvian Man as a cosmography of the microcosm. He believed the workings of the human body to be an analogy for the workings of the universe.'

Pico della Mirandola did not accept the Church's view of eternal punishment or reward: if the singular characteristic of human beings is that they change themselves, it follows that it would be impossible to lose that ability after physical death; that is, that ability would be retained in the afterlife. Eternal damnation, proclaimed by the Church, is illogical, for such damnation argues that the human soul doesn't have the power to work on its reform even after death. In the age of the consciousness soul we may say that human beings have won their independence from the gods and now take their own evolution in hand. They now have the power to develop their soul and spiritual faculties so that they may again perceive the spiritual worlds in order to gain knowledge, inspiration from the divine source. But this time, as indicated already, they will be conscious of both physical and spiritual worlds. Concerning man's relation with the spiritual world, Pico reminds us that during the fourteenth century two events had taken place which predisposed Florentines to follow Plato in making significant use of number. One was the widespread use of the mechanical clock, in which organic time was translated into mathematical units on a dial.[64] The other was the introduction of linear perspective (Brunelleschi, 1377–1446) whereby Florentine artists—as will be discussed later—pioneered the representation of objects in space in accordance with strict mathematical principles.

A major difficulty under which Florentine thinkers and scientists laboured in the fifteenth century was that they had inherited what Cronin described as 'a tangled web of fact and fantasy'.[65] Astronomy was so closely linked with astrology that the terms were interchangeable; as long as the misleading and restrictive influence of astrology prevailed little progress could be made in the fields of natural science. The following may serve as an example of the restrictive influence: Alberti, whom we shall meet again in due course, says in his book on architecture that foundations must be laid at the correct astrological moment. 'This rule was observed in 1489, when the foundation stone of the Palazzo Strozzi was laid at an auspicious time fixed by three physicians, a bishop and Marsilio Ficino, and it was observed even for churches. The position of the stars as shown in the sacristy of San Lorenzo corresponded to the heavens in Florence on 9 July 1422, when the high altar was dedicated'.[66]

In the early Renaissance, art and science were closely connected. Both the artist and the scientist strove for the mastery of the physical world. The art of painting profited by two fields of study that may be called scientific: anatomy, which made possible a more accurate representation of the human body, and mathematical perspective. In the next generation such research was carried a stage further by Leonardo da Vinci, who was born in 1452 near Florence and spent the first 30 years of his life in that city. He left upwards of 1,550 anatomical drawings, many of marvellous exactitude.

Before looking further at some aspects of Ficino's life and work, it behoves us to look briefly at the character of Lorenzo de'Medici, also known as Lorenzo the Magnificent (Il Magnifico, 1449–92). He assumed the role of his grandfather, Cosimo de'Medici in 1469, at the age of 20. Piero, his insignificant father, who was always ailing, had survived the great Cosimo by no more than four years. Lorenzo had matured early. He benefited from an exceptional education at the feet of three professors of the Accademia Platonica: Cristoforo Landino, the profoundest interpreter of Dante and Petrarch, who taught him poetics and rhetoric; Argiropoulos, the learned master of Greek, and Marsilio Ficino, who taught him philosophy and aesthetics, as well as music and poetry. He never ceased to learn, and until his death 23 years after assuming the position of power his father and grandfather had held before him, he continued to be active in the Florentine Academy and gave both encouragement and genuine support to Ficino and his colleagues at the Academy. Lorenzo's support for artists such as Donatello, Domenico Ghirlandaio, Sandro Botticelli, Andrea del Verrocchio, Leonardo da Vinci and Michelangelo Buonarroti was instrumental in the development of Florence as the epicentre of fifteenth century Renaissance Europe. Although, in contrast to his grandfather, Cosimo, his financial straits rendered it impossible for him to commission many works himself, he saw to it that they received commissions from other patrons. Towards the end of Lorenzo's life, Florence came under the powerful influence of Savonarola, who believed that Christians had strayed too far into Greco-Roman culture. Lorenzo died in 1492, at the dawn of 'the age of exploration', Christopher

Columbus would reach the 'New World' only six months later. His life coincided with the high point of the early Italian Renaissance, and his premature death marked the end of the Golden Age of Florence.

In one of his many letters to his friends and pupils, Ficino wrote that 'it was the chief work of the divine Plato . . . to reveal the principle of unity in all things.'[67] Adding the dimension of Christianity to the Platonic teaching, Ficino tended to refer to this principle of unity as God, although he also used the Platonic terms of the One or the Good. It was Ficino, more than anyone, who took from Plato, Plotinus and the Hermetic writings the concept that part of the individual human soul was immortal and divine; a concept that was all-important to the Renaissance.[68] For, from this, it followed that the power was within the human soul to become all things and that man could 'create the heavens and what is in them himself, if he could obtain the tools and the heavenly material'.[69] For Ficino the immortality and divinity of the human soul formed the foundation of 'the dignity of man', which the writers and artists of the Renaissance sought to express in countless ways. In time the expression of this ideal touched every aspect of life. The dignity of man was not only reflected in architecture and art but had to find expression in the field of human activity. A new ideal in respect of man was formed, the first and best in Ficino's view was his pupil, Lorenzo de' Medici. 'Noble, magnanimous, courageous, trustworthy, he could turn from war and affairs of state to philosophy, poetry, music or art, and excel in each. Equally at ease with his peers or his people, his authority sprang from his nature and not from his position.'[70] The impulse of the Florentine Renaissance, that the dignity, indeed, the glory, of man should be reflected in all his activities, became, in the course of time, an impulse, a movement of general refinement, which lasted for centuries, affecting the taste and manners of people throughout Europe. In particular it meant the adoption of a code of conduct by which consideration for others became a natural inclination of men and women throughout society . In origin it was the reflection of 'man's dignity' in his social behaviour. The universe, Ficino expounds, is a harmonious hierarchy of five distinct 'substances', each more particularized than its ontological predecessor. Beginning with boundless Deity, the descending order encompasses the angelic mind, the rational soul, quality and body. Man was placed by Ficino in the centre of the ladder of being. Man is, as it were, the mean between absolute spirit and primal matter. From his ontological platform man can understand the world around him and aspire to knowledge of the divine orders above him, from which he has descended. Ficino sees the human soul mysteriously linked to the World Soul, *Anima Mundi*, a microcosmic matrix of the intelligent forces of the macrocosm. The human soul's ascent of the 'ladder' of spiritual knowledge up to the Divine is not achieved without a profound and continuous effort of intellect and will energized and sustained by selfless, spiritualized love. In this work Ficino emphasizes, in addition to the divinity of man's soul, the personal relationship between man and God. Christ personifies the descent of divine love into the human realm and also represents the possibility of man's ascent to the divine. In one of his books Rudolf Steiner wrote: 'True philosophy, the love of wisdom and the wisdom of love, is one with true religion, the love that unites humanity with the divine source.' Here, Ficino would say, Plato gave the same message as Christ. The idea of love is, in fact, the very axis of Ficino's philosophical system.[71] Love is the motive power by which God causes Himself to effuse his essence into the world, 'and which, inversely, causes His creatures to seek reunion with Him'.

In the Platonic philosophy of love and beauty elaborated by Ficino, Pico and others, the main points relevant to our present study are the new emphasis on the divine origin and nature of beauty, the distinction between the heavenly and earthly Venus. Following on from earlier indications, we would emphasize here that Ficino believed that the purpose of human life was contemplation. Through conscious striving the ultimate goal was to be united with God. This goal, according to Ficino, was achieved through contemplation. At first, the human mind removes itself from the external physical world, and concentrates on abstract ideas concerning knowledge and the soul. Ultimately, an unmediated vision of God is experienced. But this final stage, according to Ficino, would be reached only after death. Grounded in this conception of contemplation that Ficino developed was a concept he called platonic love. While Ficino believed that the human soul pursued contemplation more or less in isolation, he acknowledged that human beings were fundamentally social. When the spiritual relationship between God and the individual, sought through contemplation, is 'mirrored' in a friendship, or love, with another person, that, for Ficino, constitutes spiritual or platonic love. The beauty that awoke love was always a reflection of the heavenly beauty. Venus, then, is twofold. The heavenly Venus, by innate love is stimulated to know the beauty of God; the earthly Venus, by a love of its own kind to procreate the same beauty in bodies. Each has as a 'consort' a similar love. Ficino contemplated love reaching out towards the beautiful and the good and wrote of the platonic love which can prevail between friends reaching out to God, the fountain of their friendship, in beauty and joy. The worth accorded to brotherhood, clearly placed great emphasis upon human relations.

In the naked form we see man in his full beauty. Homer, and after him, the Greek sculptors discovered the glory of the human body and gave this, the most beautiful thing they knew, to the gods; examples of this are the bronze statue of Poseidon (c.470–45 BC) at the National Museum in Athens and the marble statue of Apollo, from the west pediment of the Temple of Zeus at Olympia (465–457 BC). The Renaissance, which in this sense was indeed a rebirth, repeated this discovery.[72] The Davids by Donatello and Michelangelo bear witness to this.

In the fields of painting and sculpture it was in particular, the three Medici, Cosimo (1389–1464), Piero 1 (1416–1469) and Lorenzo (1449–1492), who, by respecting, encouraging and commissioning, enabled the traditional craftsmen to develop into free and independent creative artists. The patronage of the Medici called into being a considerable number of artistic masterpieces. Many of them were of an entirely new character. As distinct from devotional they treated secular subjects, in particular greater stress was laid on beauty. Moreover, the artist no longer followed the instructions given in medieval pattern books, but worked from his own sketchbooks in which he entered his observations and free innovations. The artistic masterpieces commissioned by the Medici filled men and women with a sense of elation and not only met with the approval but also influenced the thinking of members of the Platonic Academy. This championing of artists by Florence's most prominent citizens naturally raised their status. For instance, in his contract for the north door (1403–24) of the Baptistry, Ghiberti is explicitly described as a 'wage-earner', whereas for the east door (1425–52)—called by Michelangelo the 'Gates of Paradise'—he was dispensed from following exactly a given programme: 'I was allowed a free hand to execute them as seemed to me.' Because the works they created were now more truly their own, artists began to sign their work. This practice of representing one's self among the figures in a work of sculpture or a painting became quite common among Renaissance artists; it can be seen as a kind of signature and an expression of the artist's own conception of his significance and importance as a creative individual being.

Both Jan van Eyck and Masaccio—in his Brancacci Chapel frescoes—placed man 'at the centre' of their works. The former worked to private commissions; he produced numerous portraits of canons, princely prelates, and wealthy merchants. One day he decided to paint a picture of his wife. Not as a queen, as Eve, or as the Holy Virgin, but true to life. Her image had no value except for its author. Such a work of art indicates, in no uncertain terms, that the artist attained his independence.[73] Cronin makes the point that it is important to differentiate between the rise of the individual in Florence and his rise elsewhere in Italy in the fifteenth century. In Florence the community minded individual was particularly to be found to be a creative artist or philosophic thinker, elsewhere, more often than not, he, the individual, took the form of the feudal despot, who set himself apart, outside the community, by his unbridled passion for power and fame.[74] 'It is the mark of the fifteenth century that the Florentine artist became an individual without outgrowing his strong civic sense, or forgetting Ficino's dictum that man proves himself a member of the human race by loving other men as his equals, by being humane.'[75]

If we were ever to become so utterly materialistic as to lose our sense of meaning in life, and dignity in man, art would die, for it cannot exist without idealism. A living art is an enemy to materialism and encourages man's mind to other than material values. The creative artist values the sacred rights of the individual. In a totalitarian state freedom, personality, conscience and individual happiness are sacrificed in the great impersonal 'machine'. Those soul qualities are the very essentials of his art—freedom and the urge, the right to rebel against what he holds to be evil. The tendency to ignore the essential individuality of the separate human being, to deal in men and women as an amorphous mass, and to categorize them, organize them in accordance with doctrinaire conception can but be inhuman. Creative, imaginative art is the expression of one individual's hopes, beliefs, visions, observations, addressed to the sensitivity and response of other individuals.

In the first chapter of the third book on architecture Vitruvius makes the momentous statement: man's body is a model of proportion because with arms and/or legs extended it fits into those 'perfect' geometrical forms: the square and the circle. This declaration, and others by Vitruvius, dovetailed neatly with Plato's teaching that the structure of reality, as well as beauty, are geometrical. They were therefore adopted and formed the basis of much Florentine architecture during the fifteenth century. Proportion, whether in the human physical body or in a building, particularly a church, was regarded as the distinctive mark of beauty and a reflection of God's cosmic order.[76] The conviction that architecture is a science, and that each part of a building has to be integrated into one and the same system of mathematical ratios, may justifiably be called the basic axiom of

Renaissance architects. Architects have been led to experiment with circular or octagonal plans, in which the holy table stands at the centre of the building. The architect, Sir Frederick Gibberd (1908–1984) conceived the building of the fourth Roman Catholic Cathedral—the Metropolitan Cathedral of Christ the King, Liverpool—as a huge circular space the focus of which is the centrally placed altar. Building began in October 1962. Less than five years later, on the Feast of Pentecost, 14 May 1967, the completed Cathedral was consecrated. The Catholic Cathedral of St Peter and St Paul in Clifton, Bristol, consecrated in 1973, also has a circular design interiorly. No one is seated far from the altar.

3. Ghiberti and Brunelleschi

In 1400 plague had swept the city of Florence. An outbreak similar to that of the Black Death (1347–50) had been feared, but, in fact, only a small number of citizens succumbed.[77] In the following year, as a thank-offering, the Guild of Cloth Merchants decided to give a pair of decorated gilded bronze doors to the Baptistry, il Battistero di San Giovanni. After holding an open competition, the syndics narrowed the field to six entrants, two of which were Florentine goldsmiths, Filippo Brunelleschi (1377–1446) and Lorenzo Ghiberti (1378–1455). He who produced the best bas-relief of a subject symbolizing Florence's deliverance, namely the Sacrifice of Isaac, would be awarded the commission. Now, how, in the year 1401, did one set about depicting the sacrifice of Isaac? In theory, the answer was simple. For several centuries mosaicists, goldsmiths, sculptors, painters and illuminators had arranged their figures—Abraham and his son, Isaac—according to an iconography portrayed in the Byzantine pattern-book, or in an earlier work so conceived, such as the mosaics to be seen in the sixth century octagonal church of San Vitale in Ravenna. Both Ghiberti and Brunelleschi show Isaac unclad. But whereas Brunelleschi shows Isaac cringing like one of the damned in a traditional Last Judgement, Ghiberti follows classical art more closely and shows the human body muscular, beautiful and proud.[78] So, after a lengthy period of over 1000 years Ghiberti reintroduced an idealized form of the unclad human body into European art. Ultimately Ghiberti was awarded the commission. He designed and cast 20 scenes from the life of Christ. In the scene showing the Resurrection he depicts Christ's body in such beauty and perfection that, as Vasari wrote,[79] it does seem glorified. The finished doors made such a favourable impression that Ghiberti was commissioned to make a second pair for the east entrance—facing the cathedral's west façade. In this second pair of doors, the east doors, Ghiberti depicts the female body with the same adherence to the classical ideal as he had shown in regard to the male body in the north door. Romanesque sculpture had not been kind to Eve; she was generally depicted as a cowering, guilty creature responsible for humankind's miserable condition, and of unprepossessing, stocky physical appearance. Ghiberti dismissed from his mind the hitherto accepted view of Eve, and drew directly on the classical conception of the beauty of the physical body. Here Eve's body is beautiful and, as it issues from Adam's rib, lifelike, seems to manifest an upward movement. Giorgio Vasari (1511–74) wrote in his *Lives of the Artists* that Ghiberti clearly intended his Adam and Eve to be the finest figures he had ever sculpted, since they had been the most beautiful creatures created by God (see Plate 1). The judges could not make up their minds whose work was superior—Brunelleschi's or Ghiberti's. Brunelleschi himself, however, recognized his fellow Florentine's superiority and withdrew his contribution from the competition. Shortly after that he and his friend Donatello went off to Rome. Brunelleschi measured and drew ruin after ruin; Donatello studied the few Roman and fewer Greek bronzes and statues that men were beginning to collect at that time. This development takes its start from group sculpture, and from the relief in particular. Individual figures are given more space for themselves. They are no longer, as in pre-Renaissance times, depicted alongside each other in a single plane, but 'step' behind or in front of each other.

Discussing the change brought about in the soul-constitution of man by withdrawal from the group-soul, Rudolf Steiner,[80] as mentioned earlier, contrasts Hector and Hamlet—'the former a strong, vigorous and co-ordinated personality . . . supported by being embedded in devotion to his family and to his ancient city, Troy; the latter capable of being as strong and vigorous and of as deep and tender a love, but thrown off his balance by being stripped by circumstances of the support of family and group and compelled to stand alone when his ego is not yet sufficiently mature for such a test.'[81] In the same work to which reference was made earlier Bennell wrote: 'The new-born ego-consciousness is isolated on three levels—it is cut off from the surrounding world, from unreflexive action, and from the earlier interweaving with fellow human beings. On all three levels it looks on from without. Thus it becomes something entirely new in man's soul-history—the spectator consciousness, the onlooker . . .'[82]

Humanism, as represented in the Florentine Academy, attracted to itself the finest talents and brains, and thereby, no doubt, did little to encourage an inductive investigation of nature. However, at the close of the fifteenth century, Italy, with such individualities as Paolo Toscanelli (1397–1482), and Leonardo da Vinci (1452–1519), held a very high place among European nations in mathematics and the natural sciences.[83] Toscanelli was a mathematician, geographer and astronomer. He was a friend of Christopher Columbus (1451–1506), and Leonardo's teacher in mathematics and geography. For Leonardo the greatest function man could fulfil was to endeavour to understand the natural world, not to indulge in what was, to him, a kind of abstract speculation rife among certain Florentine philosophers of his day, that is to say, the philosophers who adhered to the ideas of Plato. For the Florentine Neoplatonists, such as Ficino, the highest truth could be obtained by a mystical ascent of the human mind towards the divine realm, the spiritual world. The physical senses play little if any part in this. As the Christian Platonist, St Augustine of Hippo (AD 354–430) wrote: 'Do not go out: return into your own self. The truth resides within man himself.' And Pico della Mirandola wrote that sensory knowledge 'is imperfect knowledge, not only because it requires a brute and corporeal organ, but also because it only attains to the surface of things. It does not penetrate to the interior, that is to the substance, but is vague, uncertain and shifting.'[84] The Platonists' quest for truth within man's soul was denounced by Leonardo, he clearly believed that the 'knowledge' which the Platonists claimed to possess could never be verified against objective truth, because what they claimed to be knowledge could only 'begin and end in the mind'.[85] 'All science will be vain and full of errors which is not born of experience, mother of all certainty. True sciences are those which experience has caused to enter through the senses, thus silencing the tongues of the litigants.'[86] Leonardo saw no mutually exclusive polarities between science and the arts.

Looking again at landscape painting: the precursor of Renaissance landscape painting in Italian was Giotto di Bondone (1267–1337) who was born near Florence. But it was the new generation of artists in the fifteenth century, such as Masaccio (1401–28), Piero della Francesca (1416–92) and Leonardo da Vinci (1452–1519) that carried the development to new heights. However, for the first creation of realistic landscapes in Renaissance painting we have to turn to northern Europe, to Flanders, to the exquisite and detailed renderings of the van Eyck brothers, to Hubert (d.c.1426) and, in particular, to his younger brother, Jan. (d.1441).

The Florentine community of the fourteenth century had succeeded in preparing the site for the cathedral of Santa Maria del Fiore; a number of nearby buildings were demolished so as to open up clear vistas of the cathedral; surrounding roads were widened so that it could be encircled by spacious streets. The vast dome of the cathedral, constructed in accordance with Brunelleschi's drawings and under his personal supervision, with its curved silhouette, does not relate only to the quarters and streets which radiate from it, but also to the hills surrounding the town.

The great dome was looked upon by the Florentines of the fifteenth century as the city's crown, for in the third decade of that century Florence, having conquered most of its neighbouring towns, became the capital of Tuscany.

Earlier we saw how, in sculpture—and we shall see the same occurring in painting—individuals 'stepped out' of bondage to a group, that is, emerged from the group-soul experience to that of consciousness of self, to that of *consciousness*. Man began to find his own individual space; we could say, an interior space in which he could find and be himself. In this context, Gottfried Richter wrote:

> If any pathological or abnormal state of consciousness threatens us with loss of the sense of self we instinctively cling to our sense-perceptions of the physical world around us to restore us to ourselves—to give us again a sense of security. Hence any development that takes us out of the seeming security of the solid, sense-perceptible world without giving us anything adequate in its place, could only be viewed with misgiving.[87]

Earlier it was mentioned that man's recognition of himself as separate from the world in the age of the consciousness soul was an essential preliminary condition for the achievement of freedom and egohood. Consequently the world, having become an 'outside' object, is no longer linked to man as it was in the consciousness of earlier ages. Man's attitude, in short, becomes necessarily a distance-keeping one, a *cold* one. When we consider the world and everything in it, including men and women, to be things, objects, we cease to have any *warm* relationship with them in our life of soul. It is a primary task of the consciousness soul to overcome this coldness, to change the cold, dead thinking of the intellect into the warmth of living thinking illuminated by the spirit (see what was mentioned above in connection with King Lear's youngest daughter, Cordelia). It is our task today to forge new links with the external world, links that are created by the activity of our own 'I', so that we no longer simply *know* the world (or think we know it), but *love* it. It is an essential part of our living thinking that we connect ourselves with the world and our fellow human beings in our feeling life of soul. The poet and scientist, Goethe, expresses this thought very succinctly in his epic play *Faust* when he has Mephistopheles state that the objective, cold-blooded scientist, devoid of feeling, would never be able to understand life:

> He who would study organic existence,
> First drives out the soul with rigid persistence;

Then the parts in his hand he may hold and class,
But the spiritual link is lost, alas![88]

It has been made clear already that it was, and still is, the proper task of the consciousness soul age to come to terms with the material world. To do this man has to be able to observe it objectively, that is, stand as it were a short distance from it and observe it. Yet this withdrawal from the world in order to look at it carries with it a certain danger. The objective observer can, and often does, become cold and loveless in relation to what he sees. Steiner has pointed out how the developing intellect of the consciousness soul was *at first* necessarily cold, while the ability itself was being acquired. But Steiner also emphasized that this attitude must not continue too long. On the contrary, man should *warm* his thinking. But this must be by his own free deed. To state this quite flatly, love must come to be a means of cognition.[89] The human being needs to strive to connect himself with the outside world, including his fellow human beings *by his own* act, that is, not imposed upon him by any 'outside' influence, and this act needs to take place not only in the realm of rational thinking but also in that of feeling, of loving the world. Eventually, this union of 'head' and 'heart' brought about by a free act, will make possible the perception of the supersensible element in all things, that is, the beings of the hierarchies who are active within them. The consciousness soul, Rudolf Steiner makes this quite clear, must courageously and diligently acquire the ability to perceive the beings of the spiritual worlds—as the sentient soul of, say, the initiated in ancient Egypt did without any effort of its own. So, it is the task of the consciousness soul era to recover perception of the spiritual worlds which was still strong in the sentient soul era, the era of the ancient Egyptians, the Chaldeans and Babylonians. But the knowledge thus gained will not be reacquired in the same form as then. If it is reacquired it will be done *consciously*, and the ability to both perceive and understand the physical world from a material point of view will not be lost. So, according to Rudolf Steiner, humankind will have regained knowledge of the world of the gods, the spiritual world, that the sentient soul in its time had, should the consciousness soul achieve its goal.

4. The Platonic Academy in Florence—Ficino and Pico

> All that we regard as the norm of Western European art—Botticelli's paintings, Monteverdi's music, Shakespeare's philosophical lovers—has flowed from Ficino's Florence.
>
> *(Kathleen Raine in* The Times*)*

> Society works best ... and men are happier, when the assumption is made that the human being has an inherent dignity that must not be violated.... We can say of this concept of human dignity that it is a philosophical bastion of the free world.
>
> *(Russell W. Davenport;* The Dignity of Man*)*[90]

In the first of five lectures Rudolf Steiner gave on *The Bhagavad Gita and the Epistles of St Paul* (28 December 1912–1 January 1913) he tells us that during the first 1000 years of the Christian era Greek life unconsciously streamed into the Christian civilization and that during the following 1000 years Greek life will have to be absorbed more and more consciously. 'In every soul there will be a spiritual life in which Hellenism and Christianity flow together.' Ernst Troeltsch (1865–1923), a German Protestant theologian and writer on the philosophy of religion and philosophy of history, wrote: 'I do not doubt that the synthesis of Neoplatonism and Christianity will once more be dominant in modern thought.'[91] In the quattrocento, the fifteenth century, in Florence, we see a unique constellation of thinkers and artists, who turn to ancient Greece. Learned Greeks, such as Bessarion (1403–1472), participated in the Council of Florence* and Georgius Gemistos Plethon (c.1355–1450), who accompanied the Emperor John VIII Palaeologus. However, instead of attending

* Facilitated by Cosimo de'Medici, at which a proposed union of the Greek and Roman churches was discussed.

the Council Plethon spent his time discoursing on Platonism and Zoroastrianism to the Florentines among whom was Cosimo de'Medici. Enthusiastic Florentine listeners soon began to study Greek. Cosimo encouraged this full-heartedly. It was Plethon's enthusiasm for Platonism that influenced Cosimo to found a Platonic Academy at Florence. Cosimo's special protégé was a sensitive 18-year-old youth, Marsilio Ficino, the son of his court-physician. Above all, Ficino immersed himself in Plato's writings. He translated many books for his patron, Cosimo de'Medici, (Plato, Plotinus, Jamblichos, Proclus, Porphyrios), and was soon teaching and lecturing in public. He warmly expounded Plato's philosophy. There he found not only a wonderful synthesis of the whole pre-Platonic wisdom but also the seeds of Christianity. Indeed, he thought—and this can be clearly discerned in his writings—that Plato's teachings could lead to a better understanding and deepening of Christianity. The idea of founding an academy after the pattern of Plato's Academy in Athens most likely arose as a consequence of numerous discussions and close cooperation between Cosimo de'Medici and Marsilio Ficino. It could be said of Cosimo de'Medici, that he made his most significant contribution to the arts through his patronage of humanist libraries. His three major library initiatives were charitable activities and included Italy's first *public* library.[92] With Cosimo's active involvement, San Marco became Italy's first public library. Designed by Michelozzo di Bartolommeo (c.1396–1472), it was 'a miracle of grace and light'[93] from the day it opened in 1444. Dale Kent writes:

> It was the library . . . [in which] the architect's talents and Cosimo's style of patronage most effectively converged. The library—cool, classical, spare, and graceful . . . is the architectural masterpiece of San Marco. The austere character of its design mirrored the character of its patron . . . The quality of the library also expressed the quality of Medici literary friendships. Cosimo . . . was chiefly responsible for making Niccolò de'Niccoli's legendary humanist library the nucleus of his own donation. The library became a gift to the city as well as to the church, since by Niccoli's wish his books were to be freely available to all Florentine laymen.[94]

In the early 1460s Cosimo also built and furnished a convent library at the Badia in Fiesole. His first library endeavour was outside Florence, it was a gift in return for the Venetian hospitality he enjoyed during a short exile. It was built and furnished in 1433 for the San Giorgio Maggiore monastery in Venice.

We should note that although the Accademia Platonia at Florence also strove to achieve a synthesis of Platonism and Aristotelianism it is *clear that the Aristotelian stream was not always given due significance.*

We do find such a synthesis expressed by Raphael in the fresco in the Vatican, *The School of Athens*, painted between 1508 and 1511. This is one of the most revealing masterpieces of Italian High Renaissance art. It shows Greek philosophers arranged in different groups according to their philosophical inclinations. In the centre stands Plato, pointing upward indicating his commitment to his theory of Ideas, and Aristotle, pointing downward to indicate his empirical orientation. The left side of the picture shows metaphysical thinkers (Socrates and others), and on the right side are the representatives of the physical sciences. This painting may be regarded as a tribute to Greek philosophy, which, as is clear from these pages, played such an important role in the Italian Renaissance. Here we should remember that two other great artists and thinkers, Michelangelo and Leonardo da Vinci, from whom Raphael learnt much, had to a greater or lesser degree been familiar with Neoplatonic philosophy as propounded by Ficino and Pico. It was in the Medici household that Michelangelo received his early education, and he was no doubt familiar with Ficino's works and his translations of Plato and Plotinus. Michelangelo's philosophy of art was Neoplatonic. For instance, he believed that the artist's function was to bring pre-existent forms out of the material at hand; 'the greatest artist has no conception which a single block of marble does not potentially contain within its mass, but only a hand which obeys the *intelleto* can accomplish that'.[95] Art forms, or the *concetto*, exist independently of the artist, and are implanted in matter by nature. The artist's function was to draw these forms out of the material. Some artists, however, were more skilled than others, since they had the ability to perceive harmony and beauty, or an *intelleto*. This ability, or *intelleto*, was a gift from God. Michelangelo wrote in one of his poems: 'As a sure guide to me in my vocation, the idea of beauty, which is a mirror and a lamp to both my arts, was bestowed upon me at birth. Whosoever conceives otherwise is mistaken. This idea alone lifts my eyes to those high visions which I set myself to paint and carve here below'.[96] Michelangelo was able to harmonize the design of a statue with the proportions of the block of marble. This ability was a gift from God, and those who possess *intelleto* did not need to rely on artificial techniques to create a work of art.

Michelangelo differed in this respect from many Renaissance theorists, including Leonardo da Vinci, Ghiberti and Alberti, who argued that art should reproduce nature. Michelangelo's conception of the *concetto* and *intelleto* was in opposition to such a theory.[97] The Virgin of the Rome *Pietà*, for example, appears to be even younger than her crucified Son. He also often violated the rules of perspective, making objects in the background appear larger than they should be. Of Leonardo it cannot be said that he was so clearly influenced, but, as Martin Kemp succinctly states, Leonardo 'showed a more than passive sympathy with certain aspects of Platonic philosophy which colour intellectual life in the Medici circle'.[98] Raphael was acquainted with members of a circle of thinkers and artists who discussed philosophy and who, in contrast to the Florentine Academy, gave equal 'weight' to the Platonic and Aristotelian points of view.[99] The location in the Vatican of Raphael's fresco *The School of Athens* is revealing for, facing it on the opposite wall, is his *Disputà*, which depicts a disputation, a debate regarding the mystery of transubstantiation by which Christ's presence in the Eucharist is effected. The placement of these two frescoes expresses the values characteristic of the Italian Renaissance acknowledgement of pagan culture without rejecting Christianity. In Raphael's frescoes in the Stanza della Segnatura the four themes of Theology, Pagan Philosophy, Poetry and Justice are clearly blended.[100]

5. Humanism

> Whatever the particular conditions that coincided with the apogee of Greek civilization, it favoured a greater clarity of the intellect than had ever been seen before. . . . Today we show little sign of understanding the conditions that produced it or the true nature of this clarity. It was an inspired lucidity of vision that reappeared in the Renaissance; in the present century clarity is confused with mechanistic reason. This confusion can perhaps be seen as an aspect of the disturbance and clouding of the modern mind, for it should have been evident that reason, without a humanizing predisposition, can but end as a dehumanizing agency, as is proved by the humanly insensitive application of science.[101]
>
> *(Frank Avray Wilson)*

Humanism, an educational and philosophical outlook that emphasizes the personal worth of the individual and the central importance of *human values* as distinct from religious belief, blossomed in Florence during the fourteenth century (Petrarch, 1304–1374, and Boccaccio, 1313–1375, and Coluccio Salutati, 1331–1406) and, in particular, in the fifteenth century, influenced by the study of Latin and, above all, ancient Greek literature and philosophy. Humanism thus began as an educational programme called the humanities,[102] which inculcated those ancient secular values consistent with Christian teachings. The Renaissance humanists were often devout Christians, but they promoted secular values and a love of pagan antiquity. The Italian Pietro Paolo Vergerio (1349–1420) was the author of the most influential Renaissance tract on education.[103]

> 'The spiritual substance of Renaissance Humanism was Christian as the spiritual substance of ancient Humanism was pagan, in spite of the criticism of the pagan religions by Greek Humanism and of Christianity

by modern Humanism', wrote Paul Tillich in his eye-opening book *The Courage To Be*.[104]

During the Middle Ages little attention was paid to Humanism, but, with the beginning of the Renaissance there was a revival of that perspective. Renaissance Humanism was both an outlook and a method. It has been described as 'Man's discovery of himself and the world'. The worth of earthly existence for its own sake was accepted, and the otherworldliness of medieval Christianity was disparaged. Rudolf Steiner makes a statement in this connection which is of relevance here. The European race in particular, with its strong sensory orientation must apply itself to the task of finding a way to the spirit through the senses.[105] Humanism, as it prevailed in fifteenth century Florence, replaced the medieval view of humanity as fundamentally sinful and weak with a new and confident view on humanity's innate moral dignity and intellectual and creative potential. (See 'The Dignity of Man' below.) Closely allied to the new view of worldly life was a devotion to the beauty of the human physical form and that of the world of nature; many Renaissance artists bear witness to this. It should, of course, also be mentioned that those who were actively involved in the movement were devoted to the *studia humanitatis*, or the liberal arts.

As stated earlier, among the first Englishmen to visit Italy and to come under the influence of Florentine Humanism was William Grocyn. He studied Greek and Platonic philosophy under Demetrius Chalcondyles (1424–1511), who had been called to Florence by Lorenzo de'Medici in 1479; and Angelo Poliziano (1454–1494). Thomas Linacre (c.1460–1524), after whom Linacre College, Oxford is named, was also one of the earliest Englishmen to study Greek in Italy. He brought back to his Oxford university the lessons of the 'New Learning' and formed a circle of brilliant scholars which included William Grocyn and John Colet (1467?–1519).[106] Among his pupils was Desiderius Erasmus (c.1469–1536), the Dutch humanist and scholar.[107]

Erasmus was the most influential of the Christian humanists. In his *Colloquies* and *The Praise of Folly* he satirized the corruptions of his contemporaries, especially the clergy, in comparison with the teachings of the Bible, early Christianity, and the best of pagan thinkers. In his *Adages*[108] he showed the consistency of Christian teachings with ancient pagan wisdom. Erasmus' friend Thomas More, described by Rudolf Steiner as 'a most significant and gifted pupil of Pico della Mirandola',[109] wrote another humanist critique of society, *Utopia* (1516), which attacked the corruptions of power, wealth, and social status. Thomas More also published a life of Pico della Mirandola. Strongly influenced by Thomas Linacre, John Colet, the founder of St Paul's School, followed in his footsteps and went to Italy, where he studied with Ficino in Florence for two years. On his return to England in 1496 he took holy orders and settled in Oxford. He later assisted Linacre in the production of the first Greek grammar book printed in England. Colet's most significant contribution to the incipient Reformation was his bold reading of the New Testament in Greek and translating it into English for his students at Oxford, which was, of course, strictly forbidden by the Church of Rome. Later, Colet went even further by reading the New Testament in English for the public at St Paul's Cathedral in London. Men and women were so hungry to hear the Word of God in a language they could understand, that, according to reports at the time, within six months there were some 20,000 people packed in the church and at least that many outside trying to get in! Colet had friends in high places, so he managed to avoid execution for such a blatant violation of the Church's 'Latin-only' policy.

Thomas Traherne (1636/7–1674), the writer and poet, studied Plato and had a knowledge of Ficino's epitomes and translations which would have conveyed to him the main doctrines of Plotinus to which Ficino refers. A notebook survives in Traherne's own handwriting with lengthy notes from Ficino's own commentaries on Plato's works. This notebook also contains Ficino's translation of *The Republic* (British Museum MS, Burney 126). Traherne was clearly not merely interested in, but also influenced by the general Christian Neoplatonic tradition of the Renaissance.

> The Dialogues of Plato and the Enneads of Plotinus have gained an almost canonical validity; they are placed on a par with the books of the Bible and treated with an equal veneration as sources of religious knowledge.[110]

Why Platonic and Neoplatonic philosophy should have had such an appeal for the Cambridge Platonists is suggested by Basil Willey:

> Here was a system, essentially religious in spirit, which taught the sole reality of the spiritual world and the immortality of the soul, which pictured life as the soul's striving for heaven and prescribed a regimen for its upward ascent: a system which was not only venerated on its

own account by the cultured but which in its long and intimate association with Christianity had flowed into the stream and become part of it.[111] (See the following chapter on the Dignity of Man.)

In the plays of Shakespeare the influence of the Renaissance, as Milward reminds us, is everywhere to be seen.[112] We may observe, for instance, that in Shakespeare's last plays 'despair gives place to hope, and the darkness of death to the light of life; and although this all takes place in a pagan setting, like that of *King Lear*, the undercurrent of thought is both religious and Christian.'[113]

In one of his letters, Ficino explains that, although we have known the heavenly harmony sounded by the movement of the planets and the constellations of the stars before we were born, we lose this ability to hear the music of the spheres because we are imprisoned, confined in our mortal physical bodies. However, we can regain this ability when love once more allows us to enter the world of the soul where, echoing the divine music created in the mind of God, we may hear:

> . . . the motions and order of the heavens, by which the heavenly spheres and their orbits make a marvellous harmony. In both of these our soul took part before it was imprisoned in our bodies. But it uses the ears of the messengers, as though they were chinks in this darkness. By the ears . . . the soul receives the echoes of the incomparable music, by which it is led back to the deep and silent memory of the harmony which it previously enjoyed.[114]

Jill Line suggests that Shakespeare surely had Ficino's words in mind when he wrote:

> Here will we sit, and let the sounds of music
> Creep in our ears: soft stillness and the night
> Become the touches of sweet harmony:
> Sit Jessica: look, how the floor of heaven
> Is thick inlaid with patines of bright gold:
> There's not the smallest orb which thou behold'st
> But in his motion like an angel sings,
> Still quiring to the young-ey'ed cherubins;
> Such harmony is in immortal souls,
> But whilst this muddy vesture of decay
> Doth grossly close it in, we cannot hear it.[115]

The soul, Ficino continues, 'Realizes that as long as it is enclosed in the dark abode of the body it can in no way reach that music. It therefore strives wholeheartedly to imitate it.'[116]

Milward draws our attention to the fact that, in Elizabethan England, the revival of Neoplatonism by the Florentine thinkers, Marsilio Ficino and Pico della Mirandola, also came to take on certain 'atheist' associations. In itself, however, as we have noted, it was a deeply religious movement; 'Platonic thought had long possessed intimate connections with Christian theology, and Ficino, as a Catholic priest, sought to renew these connections.'[117]

Erwin Panofsky pursues this theme in *Studies in Iconology, Humanistic Themes in the Art of the Renaissance*, where he states that for the Florentine Neoplatonists it was a matter of course to connect the Platonic idea of pre-existence and reincarnation with the dogma of resurrection in the Christian sense.[118] In Italian Renaissance art Neoplatonist ideas were translated into allegorical and symbolic images; images drawn from pre-Christian mythology, and interpreted as symbols for concepts acceptable to Renaissance Christians. A clear example of a work of art in this tradition is Botticelli's *Primavera*, the philosophical meaning of which is illuminatingly discussed by Edgar Wind in *Pagan Mysteries in the Renaissance*.[119]

Renaissance Humanism did not, however, spring fully evolved from classical philosophy; it emerged, as we have seen already, over a period of over a century as a fusion of Christian and classical thought.

6. The Dignity of Man

> What a piece of work is man! How noble in reason! How infinite in faculty! In form and moving how express and admirable! In action how like an angel! In apprehension how like a god! The beauty of the world.
>
> (*Hamlet* II, ii)

> Thou hast made him little less than God,
> And dost crown him with glory and honour,
> Thou has given dominion over the works of thy hands;
> Thou hast put all things under his feet.
>
> (*Psalm* 8:5–6)

> The essence of a work of art, whether human or natural, cannot be reached through intellectual analysis, rather it must be approached with a sense of wonder and awe, a state of empathy and participation must be sought. It is only when that is achieved, in whatever circumstances, that a peak experience is obtained. It needs to be emphasized, in this context, that human beings need to be recognizable as *nature's highest art of expression*; if this becomes impossible, something is very wrong with the world.[120]

Pico della Mirandola's most influential work, his *Oratio de hominis dignitate*, is a fine expression of the ideals most distinctive of Lorenzo de'Medici's Florence: freedom, versatility, the active life, and love of God through the world's beauty. Respect for the dignity of man determined Lorenzo's behaviour and all his relationships. It is said that he treated his courtiers as equals. They were free to contradict and even to correct and admonish him if, for instance, they thought that he had perpetrated an injustice. He considered his high position and the power he wielded to be a sacred responsibility. Like his grandfather he was a firm ruler, but he never became a tyrant. He endeavoured to express everything he felt and thought in poetry. Thus the thinker in him speaks in the *Altercationi*, his profoundly religious soul in the *Laudi*, and the Platonist in his love poems. Lorenzo knew the Platonic concept of 'two loves'—Sacred and Profane.[121] The Platonists saw in divine love, sacred love, a guiding spirit, the Eternal Feminine. We find her under different names in myths and poetry, and in Christianity she appears as Sophia.[122] Man, as a divine creation, was Lorenzo's favourite subject. If there were such a thing as a 'manifesto' of the Italian Renaissance, Pico della Mirandola's *Oration on the Dignity of Man* would be it. No other work more thoroughly resites the human landscape to centre on human capacity and human perspective. Pico, like Ficino, was a humanist. Italian Renaissance Humanism was, inter alia, a response to the dry concerns for logic and linguistics that animated the late medieval Christian philosophy, Scholasticism. The humanists, instead of focussing their attention on what they considered futile questions of logic and semantics, focussed on the relation of the human to the divine, recognizing in human beings the summit and purpose of God's creation.[123] Their concern was to specify the place of the human being in God's plan and the relation of Man to the divine—therefore, they centred their thinking on the 'human' relation to the divine.

Plato attributes to man a power of intellection that transcends the power of reason, which can operate merely in the name of purely subjective assumptions. To gain direct experience of the realities, spiritual realities, underlying the purely subjective, Plato posits that there must be in man an organ of conscious experience that transcends the power of reason and that is capable of knowing these realities in this direct manner. He calls this higher organ of conscious experience the *nous*—the intellect; and the *nous* possesses a noetic power—a power of *noesis* (intellection)—through which it may intuit the realities of the intelligible world and hence grasp those principles in the light of which alone any true knowledge is possible.

> Plato radically distinguishes the *nous*—intellect—from *dianoia*, reason. The attribution to man of a power of intellection which transcends our power of reasoning is not unique to Plato. It is intrinsic to the thought of the Neoplatonists.[124]

Following Plotinus and Plato's *Phaedo*, Ficino treats the contemplative experience not only as the basis of metaphysical speculation since it makes certain of God's existence and of His attributes, of the intelligible world, and of the soul, but he also considers it as the only source of a true moral life. Ficino therefore maintains that the life of contemplation is the goal everyone should aim at in order to attain not only true knowledge but also moral purity. His letters contain many declamations and exhortations favouring contemplative life.

> The central concept of contemplation is also the key to a proper understanding of two other theories of Ficino that are probably the most famous among his contributions to Renaissance thought: the theory of the immortality of the soul and the theory of platonic love. The personal immortality of the soul had been accepted and taught by nearly all thinkers of the Platonist and Christian traditions and hence it is not surprising to encounter it in the thought of Florentine Platonism.... For Ficino immortality is the central dogma of Platonism, hence it constitutes the chief theme of his main work, the *Platonic Theology*, which has the subtitle 'On the Immortality of the Souls'.[125]

Kristeller states that he is of the opinion that the question of immortality became of paramount importance within the framework of Renaissance theology and metaphysics as a consequence of the *individualism* of the period, that is, of the very great importance attached to the 'concrete and *individual qualities and experiences of each human being*'.[126] Ficino's doctrine of love is discussed later in these pages.

Pico's *Oration on the Dignity of Man* opens with the words:

> I once read in the ancient writings of the Arabians that Abdala the Saracen, when asked what was most worthy of awe and wonder in the world, answered, 'There is nothing to be perceived which is more wonderful than Man.' Hermes Trismegistus[127] concurs with this view, 'O Asclepius, a great miracle is Man'.

Why a miracle? Because, Pico explains, 'Man alone is able to make his own life. Man's nature is not determined by laws or constrained between fixed limits; he is free to choose and make his own character. He can sink to the level of the brute or rise to be united with God—the choice is his, for God endowed him, from birth, with the seeds of every possibility and every way of life.' 'Imagine', Pico continues, 'the generosity of God! Man is allowed to be whatever he chooses to be! As soon as an animal is born, it brings out of its mother's womb all that it will ever possess.... Man, when he entered life, the Father gave the seeds of every kind and way of life possible.' Pico also writes in his *Oration on the Dignity of Man* about the centrality of man:

> God . . . therefore took man . . . and, assigning him a place in the middle of this world, addressed him thus . . . The nature of all other beings is limited and constrained within the bounds of laws prescribed by me. *You, constrained by no limits, in accordance with your own free will, in whose hand I have placed you, shall ordain for yourself the limits of your nature.* I have set you at the world's centre so you may more easily *observe the world* from there . . . I have made you neither of heaven nor of earth, neither mortal nor immortal so that . . . you may *fashion yourself* in whatever shape you prefer. You shall have the power to degenerate into the lower forms of life, which are brutish. You shall have the *power, out of your soul's judgement, to be reborn into the higher forms, which are divine* [my emphases].[128]

In the view of medievalists (Roman Catholic Church) human beings could never understand God because, it was maintained, nothing on earth resembled God in any way; the best that human beings could do is understand God in a negative sense—God is not like things in the sense-perceptible world. The Neoplatonists, starting with Nicholas Cusanus (c.1401–64), also adopted this view. Pico, however, reverses this situation; not only is the world similar to God, but everything that human beings can think, imagine, and create are expressions of divinity. This concept was of prime importance for art and literature in the High Renaissance; the later artists of the Renaissance, including Michelangelo, were convinced that through the operation of their own intellect and creativity they were giving expression to the divine or, at least, expressing its likeness.[129] We mentioned earlier that Shakespeare clearly reflects the Neoplatonic philosophy propounded by the Florentine Platonic Academy. He believed, with Ficino and Pico, that man could become like a god.

A description of how one may be led to true knowledge of the nature of man is given by Ficino in *De Amore* where he writes of the growth of understanding that arises from the first sight of a man's physical form, to what is perceived of that man by the reasonable mind, and finally to how, through the real vision of imagination, the true nature of man is known in the angelic mind:

> When anyone sees a man with his eyes, he creates an image of the man in his imagination and then ponders for a long time, trying to judge that image. Then he raises the eye of his intellect to look up to the reason of man which is present in the divine light. Then suddenly from the divine light a spark shines forth in his intellect and the true nature itself of man is understood.[130]

Jill Line comments here that it is from this same realm of the imagination in the angelic world that, a hundred years later, Shakespeare wrote of his own vision of the true nature of man. Hamlet may have fallen into darkness, but he was still able to speak with inspiration of the angelic world.[131] She then quotes the famous words:

> What a piece of work is man! How noble in reason! How infinite in faculty! In form and moving how express and admirable! In action, how like an angel! In apprehension, how like a god!

When Pico considers the classic humanist question as to what constitutes the dignity of man, he specifies that this dignity is to be seen in the human being's capability and freedom to be whatever he or she strives to be. Pico contends that the greatest dignity of humanity is the power of transformation, the ability and freedom human beings possess to change and express themselves in multifarious ways. This is a radical and nearly heretical departure from tradition. In early Christian, medieval and early Renaissance thought, this freedom had been lost when Adam and Eve sinned by disobeying God. Pico, however, argues that the principle virtue of humanity is that men and women are always *free* to be whatever they strive to be and express the divine in whatever way they can. Of paramount importance is the freedom of inquiry. (Such ideas about the nature of humanity and free inquiry would become the basis of the modern world view.)

Pico is one of the first European thinkers to consider the hallmark of being human to be the capacity of 'freedom'. What, we might ask, did Pico mean by it? For him, nature and spiritual beings were not free for *they* could never change themselves. If something changes in nature, it is because something else *forced* that change to come about. There are occasions when this is also true of human beings, as, for example, the process of ageing. However, it is nevertheless true to say that human beings constitute the only part of the whole of creation that can bring about changes in themselves of their own *free will*. In this connection, those who are familiar with Rudolf Steiner's book *The Philosophy of Freedom* may recollect that he wrote that human life can only have the purpose and ordering of destiny that man gives it. 'My mission in the world is not predetermined, but is at every minute the one I choose for myself.'[132]

In his *Oration on the Dignity of Man* Pico proclaims a threefold philosophy under the guidance of the three great archangels Gabriel, Raphael and Michael:

> If it be justified to speak of the mysteries, these spiritual beings may be invoked to rescue man, whose head is covered in darkness since the Fall. Gabriel, who will guide us through the wonders of nature and point out to us the omnipotence of God in nature; Raphael, the heavenly physician, who can lead us to health by moral philosophy and dialectics, which in his hand are as medicinal herbs; and finally, Michael, the high priest, who confers on us the grace of the priesthood of theology, which is like a crown of jewels.

Concerning man's relation to the spiritual world Pico writes:

> Remember the words of Asaph, the prophet: 'Ye are Gods and therewith children of the Highest'. Do not turn to ill-use the gift of the Father, which He has conferred on you in free will. Do not turn the beneficent force into a destructive one; a sacred fervour shall stream into the Spirit in order that we, dissatisfied with the middle position allotted to us, might aspire to the highest things and embrace them with all our strength—let us raise our wings in flight to the dwelling place of the Most High. There, as the sacred mysteries proclaim, the Seraphim and Cherubim occupy the first seats. We will not stay behind them, and we will not remain satisfied with the seats below them. But now the question arises: in what manner are we to reach our goal? Is there a directing line for our will? Let us rivet our gaze on the gaze of these Angelic beings and let us gaze on their life, for if we lead a life as they do—and we can do it, then our watch, or destiny, will be one with theirs.

Pico recognizes that man, by his destiny, is united with the first hierarchy. We can sense that he is 'on fire' with his cosmic vision. Elsewhere[133] Pico rounded off his picture by claiming that the universe is fulfilled by being understood by man and by attaining unity in man's consciousness. *In this sense man is the centre of the world.*

Now, we have noted that Plato proffered mathematics as a key to understanding nature. This is, to say the least, curious because Plato also passed to the Florentines a doctrine which, if strictly followed, would render such a key useless. Fundamental to Plato's teaching is that physical phenomena are not, in themselves, worth studying. The two essential elements in any natural scientific study, observation and experiment, were ruled out because the physical senses used are deceitful. It was not through the senses but through reason that the universe, including man himself, could be understood. It is apparent that the practical-minded Florentines did not heed Plato in this point, while adopting, as a working hypothesis, his interpretation of the universe in terms of a simple regular mathematical beauty.[134] Vincent Cronin draws our attention to the work of Paolo Toscanelli (1397) who was the first to carry out observation on this basis. He devoted his life to research in astronomy and geography. One problem that interested Toscanelli was movement of heavenly bodies in space. Starting from hints in Plato Toscanelli sought to break down continuous space and movement into mathematical units. One of the discoveries he made was that the equinox fell 20 minutes earlier than would follow from tables based on the Ptolemaic system. This seemingly insignificant discovery has an intrinsic and also symbolic importance. It shows a scientist, armed with Platonic hypotheses, finding that his observations disagree with Ptolemy (second century AD), the accepted authority whose astronomical and geographic work remained standard throughout the Middle Ages.[135]

It was Pico della Mirandola, the champion of human freedom, who, in his work *De Astrologia*, launched the first attack on a system that endeavoured to restrict that freedom. Pico's systematic attack on astrology had considerable importance in regard to the freedom and progress of human thought. Having accepted the Platonist view of nature as mathematical, Pico shows that the principal error underlying astrology is that it judges the activities of the human mind as if they, too, were subject to mathematical laws, but that, he asserts, is not the case. As Giannozzo Manetti (1396–1459) had shown, the new mastery of history made it quite clear that the human mind is master of time, free to move back through the centuries. Nor is the human mind subject to space, for, in imagination, a Florentine could transfer his thoughts to distant lands. Manetti died four years before the birth of Pico. He was born in Florence. He served the Florentine Republic in various offices. He is more widely known, however, for his membership of the group at the centre of the Italian Renaissance. All members of this group were committed to reviving the learning of the Greek and Roman classics and to exercising the freedom of thought that these represented. From his familiarity with the humanistic nature of classical writings, Manetti wrote a spirited rebuttal to *On the Misery of Human Life*—a book published under the name of Pope Innocent III. In this ecclesiastical work, the Church's overt disgust with the human body and human behaviour was poured forth in a torrent of invective. Manetti's *On the Dignity of Man* encapsulated the growing pride in humanity that characterized the Renaissance.

Manetti's attitude took shape in concord with a sense of personal autonomy that first was evident in Petrarch and later came to characterize Humanism as a whole. An intelligence capable of critical scrutiny and self-enquiry was by definition a *free* intelligence; parallel with individualism arose, as a favourite theme, the idea of the dignity of man. In his noted *De Hominis Dignitate Oratio* (Oration on the Dignity of Man), Giovanni Pico della Mirandola conveyed this notion with unprecedented vigour. The emergence of Renaissance individualism was not without its darker aspects. Petrarch and Alberti, among others, were aware of the sense of *estrangement* that accompanies intellectual and moral autonomy.

As with Ptolemy in the field of cosmology, it was only through observation that the Florentines progressed beyond the classical model in the field of medicine. An example: the Florentine Antonio Benivieni (c.1443–1502) composed a 'Rule of Health' for Lorenzo de'Medici, whose father and grandfather had helped to pay for his medical studies. His book, *On some Hidden and Marvellous Causes of Sickness and Healing*, completed some time after 1496, is an original work which contains some of the earliest post-mortem studies directed towards finding the internal causes of disease. But an even more fruitful revolution originated not with those trained in medicine but with certain Florentine artists. As we shall see later, following classical models, they made the naked body an important element in their art, and in order to portray it as accurately as possible, from at least 1450, regularly dissected human bodies as part of their training. Donatello's *Anatomy of the Miser's Heart* is an early work testifying to Florentine interest in the subject.

In one of his many letters to his 'unique friend' Giovanni Cavalcanti, Ficino wrote that 'it was the chief work of the divine Plato ... to reveal the principle of unity in all things'.[136] Combining the dimension of Christianity with the Platonic teaching, Ficino tended to refer to this principle of unity as God, although he also employed the Platonic terms of the One or the Good. In the same letter Ficino stated:

> [Plato] also asserted that in all things there is one truth, that is the light of the One itself, the light of God, which is poured into all minds and forms. ... This ray passes through angels, souls, the heavens and other bodies.

The divine ray, lighting beauty and inspiring love, acts as the creative power of God in forming both the macrocosm, the universe, and man, the microcosm. It also acts as a guide to those who strive to return to the source of their being. Passing through all higher worlds in our journey into creation, we take upon ourselves a corporeal body, and live in the material world. But we are also given the opportunity to discover those higher worlds of which, embedded as we are in our bodies, we may have only an occasional glimpse. As Ficino tells in his book *De Amore*, which he published in 1482,[137] creation is a love story, for, as each world is created, it falls in love with the beauty of the higher world and, from that love, a new world is created. The return journey is also through love—being the process of creation in reverse. Love is the all-essential principle which 'calls forth' the universe and holds together harmoniously all the different levels within it.

One of Ficino's contemporaries, a 'professor of Aristotelian philosophy named Agostino Nifo' (c.1473–1546) wrote of this work: 'Amplifying Plato's views on love partly by allegorizing Plato and partly by adding to him, Ficino made a not unskilful compilation of many different ideas about love.'[138]

Sears Jayne paraphrases the main argument of *De Amore*:

> The cosmos consists of a hierarchy of being extending from God (unity) to the physical world (multiplicity). In this hierarchy every level evolves from the level above it in a descending emanation from God and desires to rise to the level above it in an ascending return to God. This desire to return to one's source is called love, and the quality in the source which attracts this desire is called beauty. The human soul, as a part of the hierarchy of being, is involved in this same process of descent from God and return to God; in human beings the desire to procreate inferior beings is called earthly love, and the desire to rise to higher levels of being is called heavenly love. Human love is therefore a good thing because in both of its phases, descending and ascending, it is part of a natural cosmic process in which all creatures share. *Love is the binding force that unifies the cosmos and holds together harmoniously all the levels within it.*

One of the greatest artists of the High Renaissance, Michelangelo, already in his teens, came under the influence of the Neoplatonists of the Florentine Academy, in particular in relation to the power of love. This comes to expression not only in his poetry, but also, for instance, in his rendering of the tombs of the *Duchi*—Giuliano and Lorenzo. However, we cannot go into further detail here, and the reader is referred to Erwin Panofsky's *Studies in Iconology*.[139]

Ficino's 'rediscovery' of the immortality of the human soul was of the utmost importance in the revival of religion during the next century. In the Middle Ages it was a doctrine which had been rather neglected by Christian theologians. Through Ficino it again became central to Christian thought.[140] By decree of the Lateran Council in 1512 it was made for the first time part of the dogma of the Catholic Church. This emphasis on the *individual* soul led quite naturally to the devotional step of a 'personal relationship' with God which became so characteristic of the reformers—both within and outside the Roman Catholic church.

It would be erroneous to claim that the concept of the dignity of man was a new discovery of the Renaissance. For instance, the early Christian emphasis on the salvation of humankind and of the incarnation of Christ implied a conception of the dignity of man which, as Paul Oskar Kristeller reminds us, 'was further developed by some of the Church Fathers'. He then says:

> These ideas were never entirely forgotten during the Middle Ages. But I am under the impression that since the beginning of Renaissance Humanism the emphasis on man becomes more persistent, more systematic. . . . Petrarch, who in his unsystematic way often expresses ideas which were to be elaborated in the succeeding period, insists that nothing is admirable but the soul, and that there is only one important subject of human thought, man himself. . . . With Ficino the glorification of man assumes a more definite philosophical significance. He emphasizes mainly two aspects: man's universality and his central position. Man's universality is reflected in his relation to all parts of the universe and in his unlimited aspiration. His position in the centre of the universe, moreover, gives man an importance unrivalled by any other being except God Himself. Pico . . . modifies his theory on one characteristic point. Man is no longer the centre of the universe, but he is detached from the entire series of existing things and [as we have discussed above] free to choose his own form of life. Thus the dignity of man is no longer conceived in terms of his universality, but in terms of his liberty.[141]

For Ficino, the dignity of Man is the central element of human life on earth. For him it is the 'lens' through which all human endeavour must be seen and the criterion of all values and standards of judgement and discrimination. This fundamental characteristic of the human condition has a dual foundation: the inherent divinity of the human soul *and* its immortality. Neither feature formed part of church dogma. It was to a great extent due to Ficino's urging that the doctrine of immortality of the soul was eventually recognized, 13 years after his death, by the Lateran

Council in 1512, but the idea of the divinity of the soul was not accepted.[142] Given the dual foundation mentioned, the dignity of man implies that there is a community of evolving souls in which each *individual* is responsible for himself/herself.

Marsilio Ficino was of the view that there is only one expression of human dignity which is able to embrace its full significance: love alone can draw all individuals together and link each human being to Deity. Ficino found two of Plato's dialogues that best expressed the ageless doctrines of the ancient theologians: the *Symposium* provides a comprehensive philosophy and psychology of love, and *Philebus*, according to Ficino, 'offers an understanding of the highest good through a dialectical discussion of pleasure and the vision of eternal Good itself'.

From the time of Plutarch (c.46–c.120 AD) 7 November had been observed as being the anniversary of Plato's birthday. Ficino revived this custom for the Florentine Academy. On that day, in 1474, Ficino gathered together the 'inner circle' of the Academy to re-enact the *Symposium*. He recorded the essence of that meeting in the treatise mentioned above, *De Amore* (*On Love*). Christ is supreme love. His love is equally the active power in man and nature. In this sense man is the image of Deity. In *The Christian Religion* (*De Christiana Religione*) Ficino wrote:

> Let man revere himself as an image of the divine Deity. Let him hope to ascend again to God, even as the divine Majesty deigns in a mysterious way to descend to him. Let him love the Divine with all his heart, so as to transform himself into the Divine, who through singular love wonderfully transformed himself into man.
>
> Love appears as the herald of wisdom. If wisdom, the eternal word, the Logos, is the Son of the eternal Creator of the Cosmos, love is related to the Logos as a mother. Before even a spark of the light of wisdom can flash up in the human soul, an obscure impulse, a longing for the divine, must be present.[143]

When Ficino presented a friend with a copy of his 'Commentary on Plato's Symposium', as well as with a copy of his treatise *De Christiana Religione*, he wrote by way of explanation; 'Herewith I send you the *Amor* as I promised, but I also send the *Religio*, to make you see that my love is religious, and my religion amatory.'[144]

Love is always a 'desire' (*desiderio*), but not every desire is love. When, Pico states, unrelated to the cognitive powers, the desire remains a mere natural urge like the blind force which causes the plant to grow or the stone to fall.[145] Only when the desire, directed by the *virtùu cognitive*, becomes conscious of an ultimate goal does it deserve the name of love. This ultimate goal being that divine goodness which manifests itself in beauty. Love, Ficino declares, has to be defined as 'a desire for the fruition of beauty'.[146] This beauty is spread throughout the universe, but it exists in two forms which are symbolized by the 'Two Venuses' discussed in Plato's *Symposium*. We may note here that, under the influence of Platonism the Church fathers described God as beauty's self and the fount of beauty. Ficino frequently speaks of divine love, which he tends to identify with Christian *charitas* and with friendship. For him divine love is a spiritual bond between two persons who both participate in the contemplative life. 'For each of them, this life is a personal and individual experience, yet there is a natural community and friendship between those who pursue this ideal.'[147]

> The former Venus first embraces the splendour of divinity in herself; then she transfers it to the second Venus. This latter Venus transfers sparks of that splendour into the matter of the world [earthly matter]. Because of the presence of these sparks, all of the bodies of the world seem beautiful according to the receptivity of their nature . The beauty of these bodies the human soul perceives through the eyes. The soul again possesses twin powers. It certainly has the power of understanding, and it has the power of procreation. These twin powers are two Venuses in us, accompanied by twin loves. When the beauty of a human body first meets our eyes, the intellect, which is the first Venus in us, worships and esteems [loves] it as an image of the divine beauty, and this [the first] is often aroused to that [the second]. But the power of procreation, the second Venus, desires to procreate a form like this. On both sides, therefore, there is a love: there a desire to contemplate beauty, here a desire to propagate it.

'Each love', Ficino continues, 'is virtuous and praiseworthy, for each follows a divine image.'[148]

Titian's enigmatic allegory *Sacred and Profane Love* addresses straightforwardly the Fician Twin Venuses (*Geminae Veneres*). We may also observe that if in the case of Titian's *Sacred and Profane Love* the two modes of the soul are represented as the Neoplatonic earthly and celestial Venus, then the sarcophagus portrayed in Titian's painting may also be regarded as an appropriate metaphor of the material world as experienced by the incarnated soul.[149] (Plate 2.)

About a year after completing *De Amore* Ficino began *The Platonic Theology or The Immortality of the Soul*. This was his major work. It extended to 18 books and occupied him for five years. In proving the immortality of the soul he showed the single source and unity of two fundamental elements in the life of western civilisation, Judaic-Christian religion and Greek philosophy.[150] (The very title, *Theologia Platonica*, would not have been possible in the Middle Ages.) The monadic-triadic cosmos as described by Dionysius the Areopagite (*The Celestial Hierarchies*) is constantly referred to in Ficino's *Theologia Platonica* and *De Christiana Religione*, the two works in which he enunciated his synthesis of Platonism and Christianity, and also forms an essential element in Pico's book *Heptaplus*. Incidentally, we should remind ourselves here that the author of the *Celestial Hierarchies* was, in fact, not the Areopagite with whom St Paul spoke but an unknown author who composed, under strong Neoplatonic influence his work on nine orders of angels which he grouped into triads, each group of three representing one of the Persons of the Trinity.[151]

Over the years Ficino wrote, in Latin, copious letters which were published in 12 volumes.[152] There are a couple of paragraphs of the translators' introduction to volume I of the English translation of Ficino's letters which give us a fair idea of his significance in modern Europe and merit being quoted in full:

> [Associated] with his Academy and under his immediate influence was the most conspicuously brilliant group of men ever to have assembled in modern Europe. These were the men who embodied the Renaissance—Lorenzo de'Medici [Florence's ruler], Alberti [the architect], Poliziano, Landino [the poet], Pico della Mirandola. Directly inspired by Ficino were, among others, the great Renaissance artists, Botticelli, Michelangelo, Raphael, Titian, Dürer, and many others.
>
> It is hard to capture or define the elusive quality of spirit that not only bound so many great men in Florence to Ficino, but attracted to him, both in person and by correspondence, leading statesmen, scholars and churchmen from all over Europe. Indeed the site of Ficino's Academy at Careggi became a place of pilgrimage both during his life and after his death. The letters provide four main clues: first, the love which he extended to all who approached him; second, the wisdom which enabled him to see so clearly into the nature of his correspondents and to touch on those which could lead them to make the best of their talents; third, he seemed to understand clearly how the various activities of his correspondents related to the divine principle in man and also to their function in the state; fourth, the letters have a quality

of timelessness, so that Ficino seems to be speaking to us as clearly today as he spoke to his contemporaries in fifteenth century Florence.[153]

In his letters Ficino warns against imbalance. He speaks of disharmony within the being of man and a corresponding disharmony between the worlds of matter and spirit. Man seeks outer harmony and beauty in his possessions, but fails to harmonize in beauty 'the parts and movements of the soul'. Man must learn to 'climb into the high watchtower of the mind'. Ficino describes the constant battle between body and soul, senses and reason. How can a man be at peace with others when he is at war with himself?[154] Ficino speaks of a 'renaissance' not only of the soul but also of the body, as Michelangelo, living with the Medici family in his younger years and frequently present at Careggi, would remind us through his marble sculpture of the magnificent David (1501–1504). In this context we could also think of Donatello's bronze statue of a youthful David.

The pictorial representation of Western cultures is primarily representation of the *self.* In the foreground of European art—particularly during and since the Renaissance—stands the human form, even, as Gerardus van der Leeuw reminds us, the art of landscape painting 'could develop only by excusing its representation of nature, so to speak, through the figures of a few hunters, shepherds, or soldiers'.

One of the great accomplishments of the Greeks was their discovery of man. The sculptor Phidias (c.555–c.431 BC)[155] played just as great a role in this as did Socrates. Clothing is discarded, the human form reveals itself in its independent power. Beautiful examples of his work can be seen at the British Museum; for example, 'Theseus', from the east pediment of the Parthenon, and metopes from that temple depicting the fight between the Lapiths and the Centaurs.

When one first becomes acquainted with the early architectural structures of the Renaissance—the Pazzi Chapel and the Old Sacristy of San Lorenzo—one's initial response could well be that of disappointment, because, compared with, say, the monumental buildings of Romanesque and Gothic architecture, they are so small. They do not crush us, as it were, by their size and weight, as, for instance, Romanesque and Gothic cathedrals may be experienced as doing. We could say, and experience, that the Pazzi Chapel and the Old Sacristy, designed by Brunelleschi, are adjusted to the scale of the individual human being. The Pazzi Chapel, built by Brunelleschi about 1430 is in a style that has been called the architecture of Humanism. Kenneth Clark makes the point that these, and other buildings of the early Renaissance in Florence, are intended 'to make each individual more conscious of his powers, as a complete moral and intellectual being. *They are an assertion of the dignity of man*' (my emphasis).

The dignity of man: today these words die on our lips. But in fifteenth century Florence their meaning was still a fresh and invigorating belief. Giannozzo Manetti, a human man of action, who had seen the seamy side of politics, nevertheless wrote a book entitled *On the Dignity and Excellence of Man*. And this is the concept that Brunelleschi's friends were making visible. Round the merchants' church of Orsanmichele are life-size figures of the saints: Donatello's St Mark, of whom Michelangelo said:

> Not one could fail to believe the word of such a sincere man; and ... Donatello's St George. They show the ideal of humanity that presided over these mundane activities. The grandest of all testimonies to the dignity of man is by another member of the same group, Masaccio, in the series of frescoes he painted in the church of the Carmine. What characters they are: morally and intellectually men of weight.... They have the air of contained vitality and confidence that one often sees in the founding fathers of a civilization—the ones that come first to my mind are the Egyptians of the first four dynasties. But these men are also moved by the concept of Christian charity. As St Peter moves gravely through the streets, his shadow cures the sick. In the balancing fresco Peter and his disciples give alms to a poor woman who is one of the great sculptural creations in painting.[156]

7. The Rise and Freedom of the Artist

Up to the generation of artists which attained what Georges Duby called its 'creative majority',[157] about 1420, the visual artist—whether painter, goldsmith, sculptor or architect—played a humble role in Florence, as also elsewhere. A craftsman was strictly controlled by the regulations of his guild. If, for example, an artist was commissioned to paint a madonna he was subject to the supervision and conservative tastes of those who paid for the work. Moreover, the artist's name would only be known to those who commissioned the work. As late as 1410, in Lorenzo Ghiberti's contract with the Bankers' Guild for a statue of St Matthew, it was stated that the commission had to be fulfilled in strict accordance with the patron's wishes—'*in chel modo et forma che sia di loro piacere*'. A similar clause figured in Donatello's contract with the linen-drapers in 1419 for a statue of St Mark.

Soon, however, the Florentine artist, supported by enlightened patrons succeeded in emancipating his talents. The process differed from art to art, and in architecture was the single-handed achievement of Filippo Brunelleschi (1377–1446). He it was who, alone, had conceived the dome of the cathedral in Florence and, moreover, the structure was executed under his personal direction. He did not tolerate interference from the Guild of Masons or from any other body. The status of the architect changed when, in 1423, Brunelleschi was awarded 100 florins as '*inventore . . . della maraglia della magiore Cupola*'. He was, then designated a discoverer, that is, one who originates. When Brunelleschi died in 1446 a wax model was taken of his face, a tribute usually reserved for saints and patrons. Later, in the same century, his biography was written.

Lorenzo Ghiberti (c.1378–1455) is a clear example of the *individuality and self-consciousness* that characterize the Renaissance. He wrote the earliest known autobiography of an artist, in which his self-confidence finds vivid expression. When he had completed the eastern doors of the Baptistry in Florence in 1452, he inscribed them *Laurentii Ghibertiis mira arte fabricatum*, and even included a self-portrait and a portrait of his son, Vittorio.

The various 'strands' of the early Renaissance in Italy, in particular in Florence, did not suddenly appear out of the blue, as it were, but just, for instance, as Roger Bacon (c.1214–92), developed the concept of science long before the dawn of science per se in the fifteenth century, so also we find in Italy a sculptor, Giovanni Pisano (c.1250–1314?), who was a forerunner of the Renaissance. He heralded something new; he seems to have been the earliest artist to fight for release from the classification of artisan by his insistence on the value of his *own individual personality*. The inscriptions he left on his work, particularly the pulpit in the cathedral of Pisa, show a remarkable sense of his own worth. At the same time, in Florence, while Ghiberti was preparing to write the *Commentaries* on his work, Masaccio placed his own image among those of the apostles in the *Tribute Money*. Georges Duby, commenting on the inclusion of Masaccio's image says: 'A man's face. The other face of the freedom of the artist.'[158] When Donatello (c.1386–1466),[159] sometime between 1456 and 1460 cast, for Cosimo de'Medici, a bronze group of Judith cutting off the head of Holofernes, he signed it *Donatelli opus*. Another device was the insertion of the painter's own portrait in the right-hand corner of his canvas.[160]

Towards the middle of the fifteenth century, painters, (Piero de'Medici's' preferred art was painting), began to use the *cartellino*, a panel or label, usually painted in *trompe l'oeil*,[161] for the purpose of bearing the artist's name and signature. In Italy it appeared in the composition. An example of this inclusion can be seen in Botticelli's *Adoration of the Magi* commissioned by the Medici about 1476.

Ficino was always well disposed to the artist, for beauty played a fundamental part in his philosophy. Rejecting Plato's doctrine in *The Republic* that the arts are removed from reality, since, according to the Greek philosopher, they depict no more than external, physical objects which are themselves mere shadows of the truth, Ficino and his circle adopted a theory put forward by Plotinus, namely, that art born from love can be closer to truth than non-artistic experience. Indeed, they held that poets, painters and sculptors could succeed in probing and revealing the mysteries of existence and the universe.

Characteristic of Florentine culture, as distinct from, say, Rome, Venice, Naples, Milan, in the fifteenth century was its communal nature. How, we could ask ourselves, did the Florentine artist as a creative and independent individual fit into such a society? Leon Battista Alberti (1404–72),[162] writer and architect, gives us an insightful answer. A man, he says, is more 'human' as he differs from others, the most admirable being *l'uomo singolare*. Yet there is no contradiction, no 'conflict', between the 'singular' man, the unique individual, and the community of citizens, since, Alberti maintains, the artist, poet, architect, works for the good of his fellow citizens. 'What I write,' says

Alberti, 'I write not for myself, but for humanity'. '*Quae scribimus, ea non nobis, sed humanitati scribimus.*'[163]

It was particularly in his attitude to power and fame that the creative Florentine, at his most individual, parted company with the feudal despot and the *condottiere*. Since he was concerned to create something new, something 'beyond' himself, he set small store by his own power and glory. It is significant that no Florentine wrote his autobiography in the fifteenth century, with the exception of Alberti, whose short work was extremely modest and, moreover, written in the third person. What a contrast to another Florentine's, Benvenuto Cellini's[164] swaggering autobiography written about 100 years later (1558–62), that is, after the fall of Florence.[165]

> In art all men are not equal. Moreover art flourishes in an exciting society where hazard and even hardship act as stimulants. . . . It is even worth considering whether in a utopian state . . . art would ever achieve its highest flights at all. . . . [In] an ideal society art would die, for art, [the artist], thrives on the conflict between the ideal and the material. It is certainly doubtful whether in a Christian heaven, where all men are made perfect and there are no more tears, art could exist for a moment.[166]

Leonardo, in his *Treatise on Painting* makes it quite clear that an artist—in his illustration, the painter—doesn't just paint. He wrestles with all manor of problems and difficulties. Problems, be they of a material or spiritual nature, possess his heart and mind relentlessly. Even in moments of apparent relaxation, when he is far from his easel, his mind will be grappling with problems. A short quotation from the treatise just mentioned may serve to sum up the matter under discussion in these few paragraphs: 'The painter who paints only by rote and by ocular judgement, without bringing his mind into play, is like a mirror which imitates all things put in front of it, knowing nothing of them.'[167]

8. Vitruvius: Symmetry and Proportion

Man is all symmetrie,
Full of proportions, one limbe to
another,
And all to the world besides.
Each part may call the furthest,
brother;
For head with foot hath private
amitie,
And both with moons and tides.
(George Herbert,[168] Moon*)*

I call Architecture frozen Music.
(J. W. Goethe)

Proportion is not only to be found in
numbers and measures, but also in
sounds, weights, intervals of time,
and in every active force in existence.
(Leonardo da Vinci)

We shall consider the nature and significance of the work of this early Renaissance artist, Donatello—also of Masaccio—in greater detail in due course. Before doing so we shall need to consider two highly significant elements characteristic of early Renaissance painters, sculptors and architects: the discovery of linear perspective and the adoption of proportions, first put forward by the Roman architect, Marcus Vitruvius Pollio, generally known as Vitruvius (first century BC), in his treatise *De Architectura.* For centuries, the detailed instructions Vitruvius gives in the *Ten Books of Architecture* were to a large extent followed throughout the time spanned by the Roman Empire. After the fall of the Empire in 476 AD, 'barbarian' forms of architecture were introduced, and the canonical instructions of Vitruvius more or less ignored. After nearly a millennium of obscurity, the rediscovery of his works around 1410 heralded the renaissance in architecture. The greatest architects of the Renaissance in Italy, including, in particular, Brunelleschi, Donato Bramante (1444–1514), Michelangelo Buonarroti (1475–1564); Iacopo Barocci (Il Vignola; 1507–73) and Andrea Palladio (1508–80), were all students of

Vitruvius's work, most of their masterpieces were based on the proportional systems enumerated by Vitruvius. He saw a building's design in terms of the body of a man. The well-known designs which show a man's body superimposed on geometry (the pentagram, for example) are known to this day as Vitruvian man.

Western classical architecture, such as that of Greece and Rome considered the circle, the square, and the triangle to be the most perfect of building forms. These geometric forms are directly expressed in architecture, especially in Italian Renaissance religious structures. In Greece and Rome the same forms were used as the measure of the perfect human body. This belief was revived during the Renaissance and was the subject of several drawings by Leonardo da Vinci. Leonardo based his drawing on some hints at correlations of ideal human proportions with geometry in Book III of the treatise *De Architectura* by Vitruvius. Leonardo's drawing (Plate 3) depicts a nude male figure in two superimposed positions with arms and legs apart and simultaneously inscribed in a circle and a square.

However, not all Vitruvian architecture is related to the proportions of a man's body. This is largely relevant for the temple or similar structure. The construction of the theatre, first described in writing by Vitruvius, demonstrates its nature as a microcosm of the macrocosm, of the world. This idea was later taken up in the Renaissance and enshrined in the famous words uttered by Jacques in Shakespeare's *As you Like It* 'All the world's a stage . . .'. The theatre in which these words were, in all likelihood, uttered for the first time was aptly named The Globe![169]

In the first chapter of the third book on architecture Vitruvius makes the following statement:

> Without symmetry and proportion no temple can have a regular plan; that is, it must have an exact proportion worked out after the fashion of the limbs of a finely-shaped human body. For Nature has so planned the human body that the face from the chin to the top of the forehead and the roots of the hair is a tenth part; also the palm of the hand from the wrist to the top of the middle finger is as much; the head from the chin to the crown, an eighth part. . . . In like manner the various parts of temples ought to have dimensions answering suitably to the general sum of their whole magnitude. If you set your legs so far apart as to take a fourteenth part from your height, and you open and raise your arms until you touch the line of the crown of the head with your middle fingers, you must know that the centre of the circle formed by the extremities of the outstretched limbs will be the navel, and the space

between the legs will form an equilateral triangle. The span of a man's outstretched arms is equal to his height.[170] (See Plate 3.)

Vitruvius also referred to the circle as one of the two perfect forms.[171] For Plato it was the most perfect shape of all. Ficino regarded the circle as the most appropriate symbol of God, who is both centre and circumference of the circle. God expresses himself in the cosmos, states Leon Battista Alberti through circular forms. For this reason it seemed that a building devoted to the worship of God should have a circular form. Peter Hammond in *Liturgy and Architecture*, published in 1960, wrote of the church of St Engelbert, Riehl, in the northern part of Cologne, which was consecrated in 1932:

> The plan of St Engelbert's, Riehl is founded on a perfect circle. The high altar is set in the midst of a shallow sanctuary opening off the circular nave, from which it is approached by a broad flight of steps ... Though churches based on the circle or the ellipse have become common enough during the past ten years, this is the first convincing example of a modern church with a plan of this type.[172]

Hammond draws our attention to the fact that during recent years many clergy and Renaissance artists firmly adhered to the Pythagorean concept 'All is Number' and guided by Plato and the Neoplatonists, and supported by a chain of theologians from Augustine onwards, they were convinced of the mathematical and harmonious structure of the universe. 'This implies', Wittkower points out, 'that if a church [for instance] has been built in accordance with essential mathematical harmonies, we react instinctively; an inner sense tells us, even without rational analysis, when the building we are in partakes of the vital force which lies behind all matter and binds the universe together.'[173]

According to Pythagoras, simple numbers and their mutual relations, as well as the simple geometrical figures that obey such measures, represent the innermost secret of nature. Every individual thing which exists, no matter how complex it may be, is 'made up of the geometric building stones'. The human body came to be considered the revelation of perfect measure. 'For without symmetry and proportion', to quote Vitruvius again, 'no temple can have a measured composition; that it must have the exact measure of the members of a well-shaped human body.'[174] 'Once an ideal human figure, which obeyed the demanded simple numerical measurements, had been constructed, it served in turn to prove the sanctity of the canon: the law of the cosmos could be read off from that of

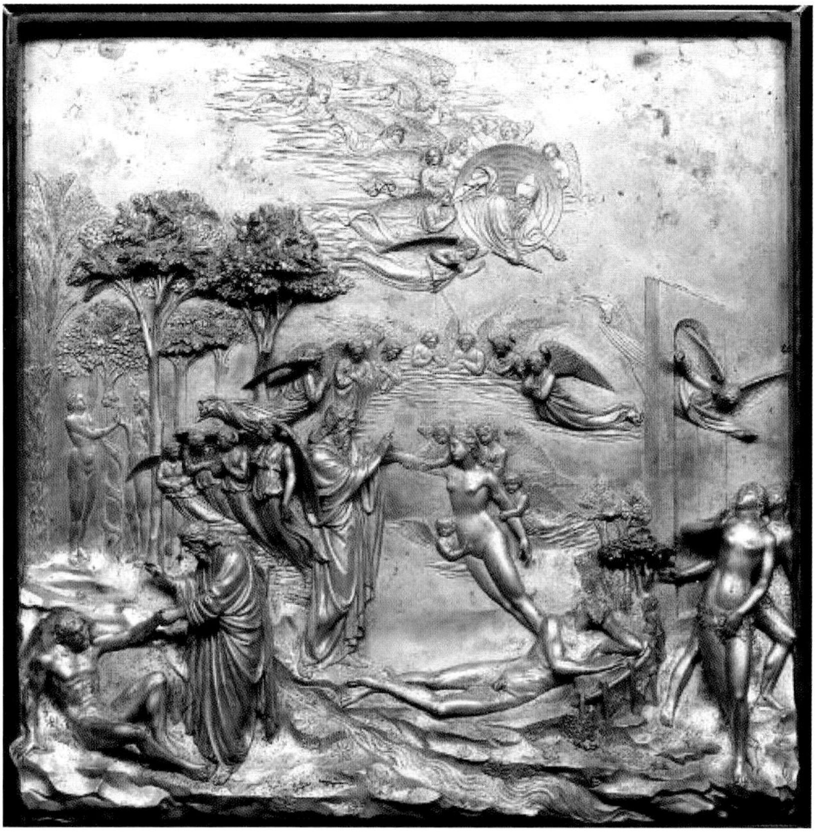

1. *Lorenzo Ghiberti: Creation of Eve (Panel on east door of Baptistry, Florence)*

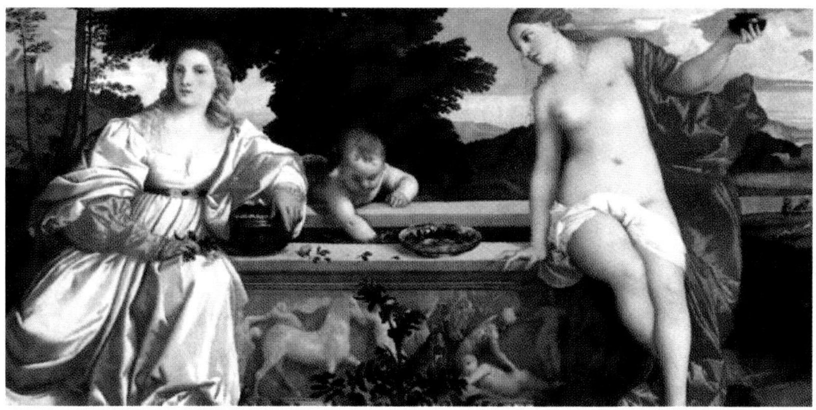

2. *Titian: Sacred and Profane Love (Museo Galleria Borghese, Rome)*

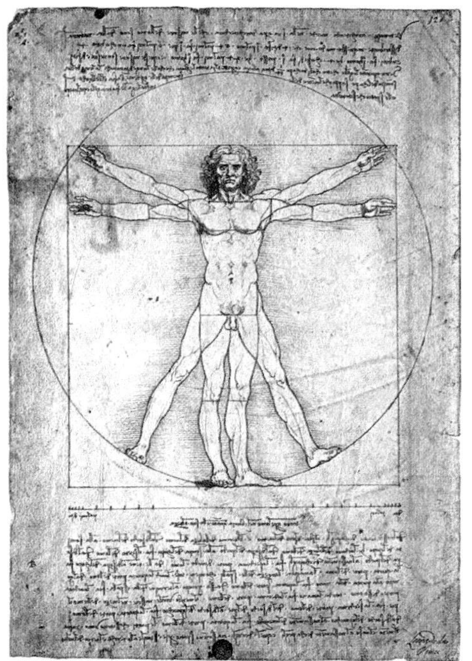

3. Leonardo da Vinci: Vitruvian Man (A drawing in one of his notebooks)

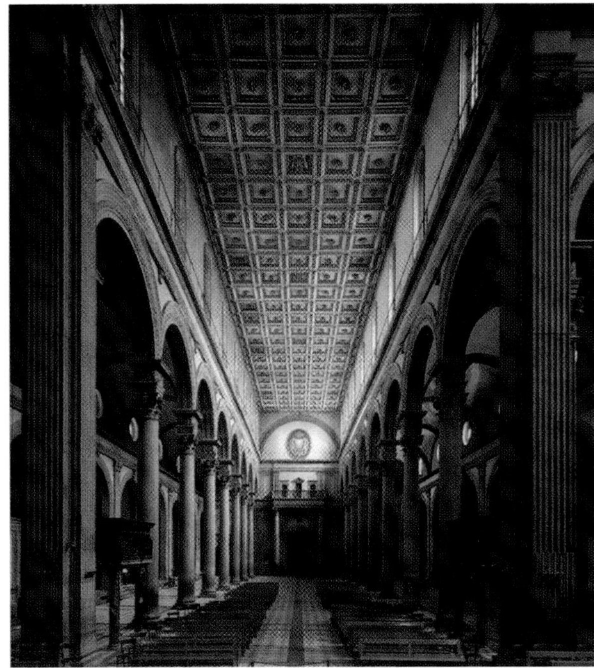

4. Brunelleschi: Interior of San Lorenzo Church (Florence)

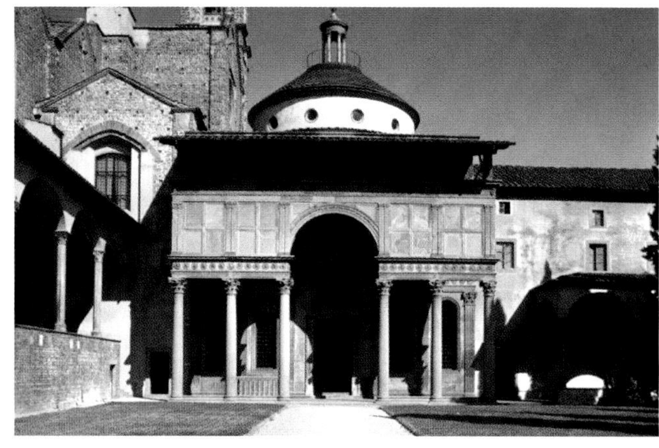

5. Brunelleschi: Facade of the Pazzi Chapel (Florence)

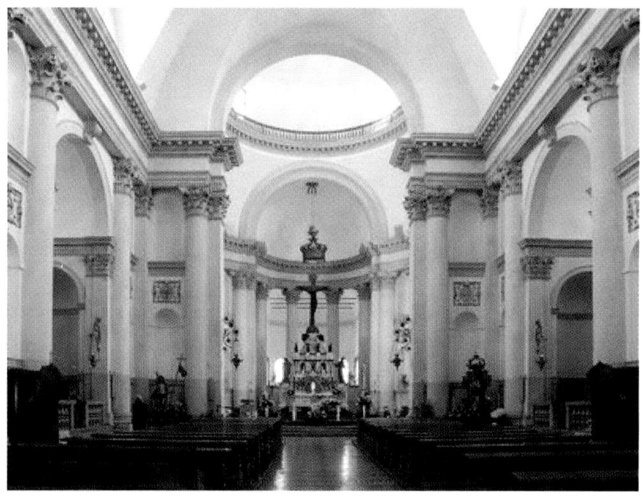

6. Andrea Palladio: Interior of Redentore Church (Venice)

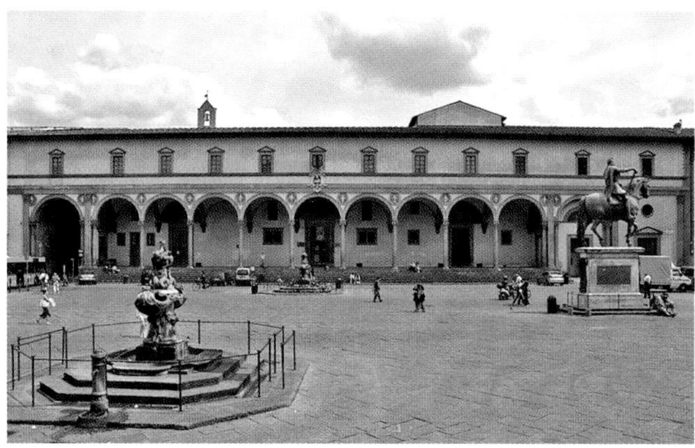

7. Brunelleschi: Facade of the Ospedale Degli Innocenti (Florence)

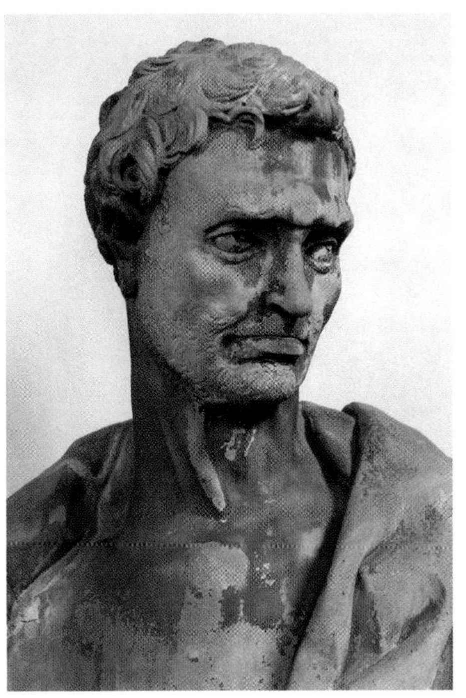

8. *Donatello: Prophet Jeremiah, detail (Museo dell'Opera del Duomo, Florence)*

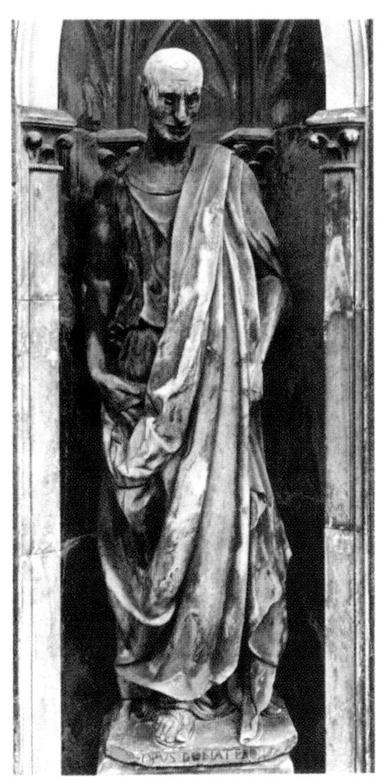

9. *Donatello: Zuccone (Museo dell'Opera del Duomo, Florence)*

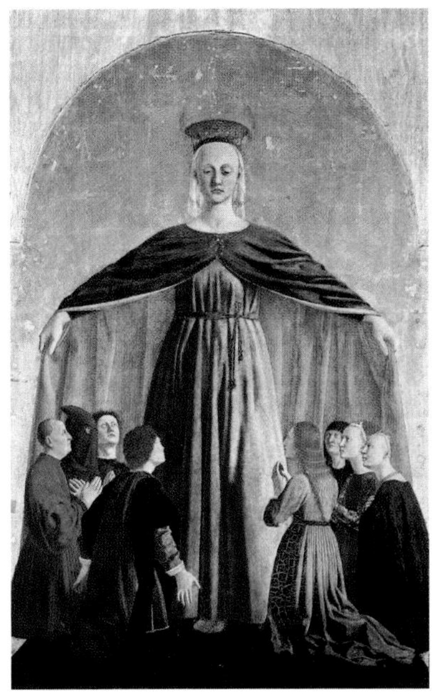

10. *Piero della Francesca: Maria Della Misericordia (Main panel of Polyptych. Pinacotecca Communale, Sansepolcro, Tuscany)*

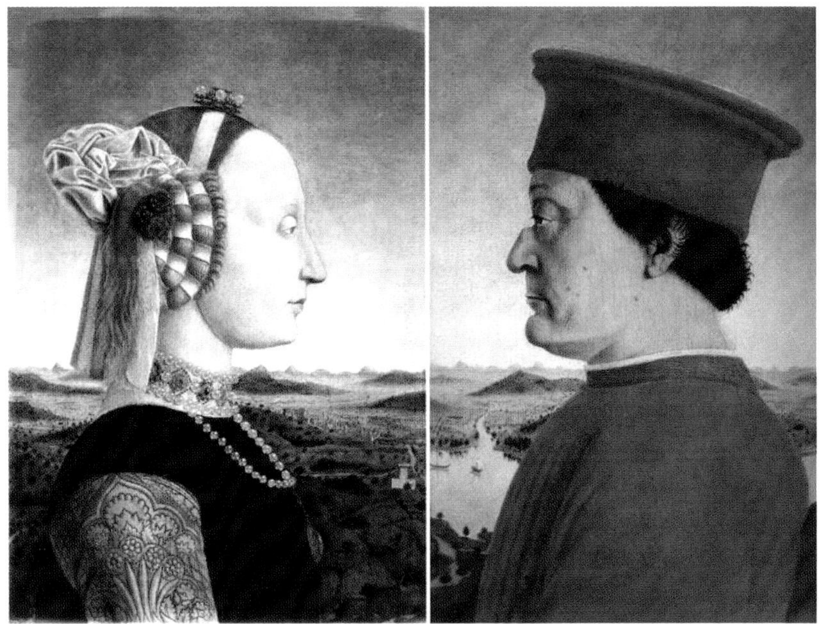

11. Piero della Francesca: Portraits of Battista Sforza and Federico da Montefeltro (Galleria degli Uffizi, Florence)

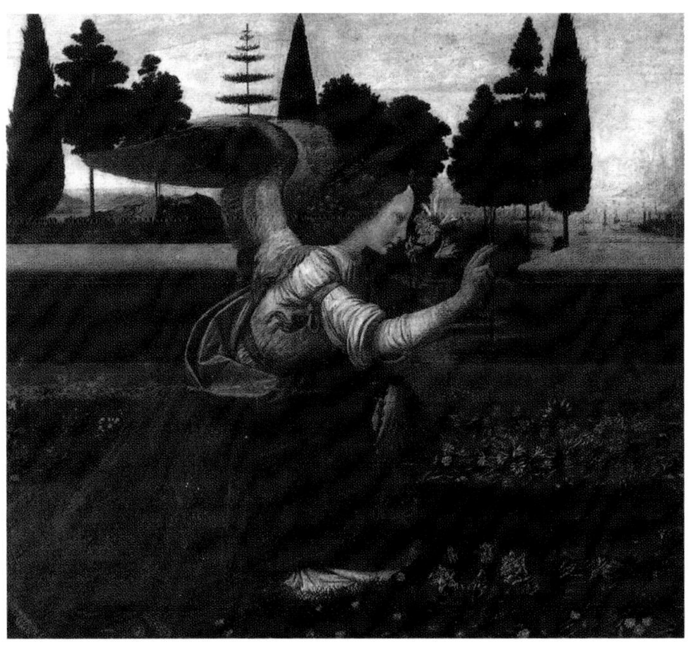

12. Leonardo da Vinci: The Annunciation, detail (Galleria degli Uffizi, Florence)

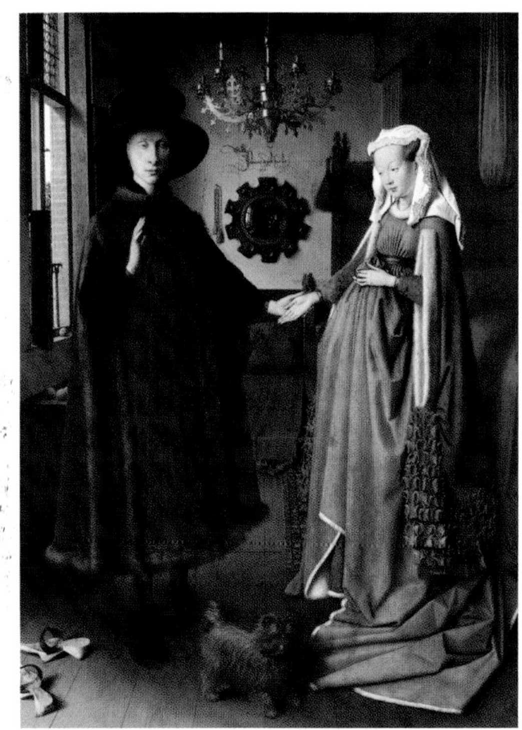

13. Jan van Eyck: The Betrothal of Giovanni Arnolfini and Jeanne de Chenany (The National Gallery, London)

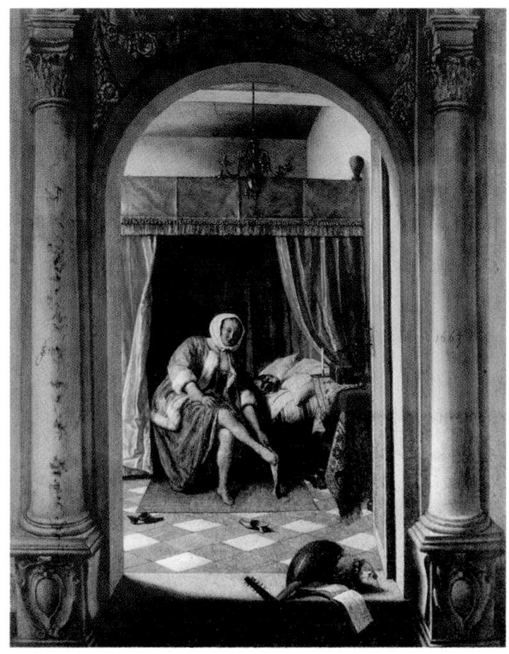

14. Jan Steen: A Woman at her Toilet (Rijksmuseum, Amsterdam)

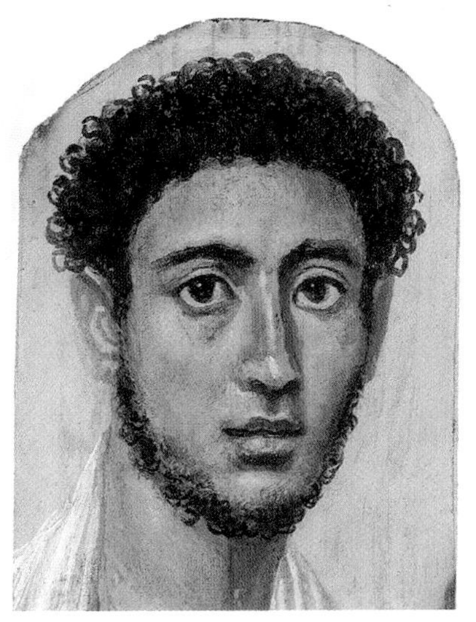

15. A Fayum Mummy portrait

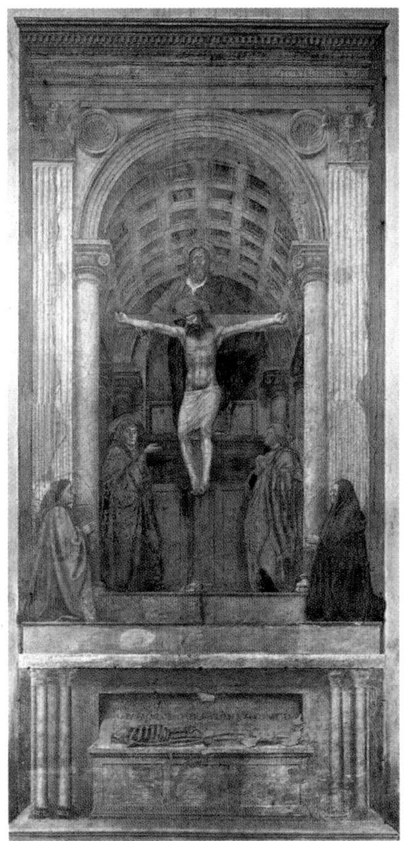

16. Masaccio: The Holy Trinity (Santa Maria Novella Church, Florence)

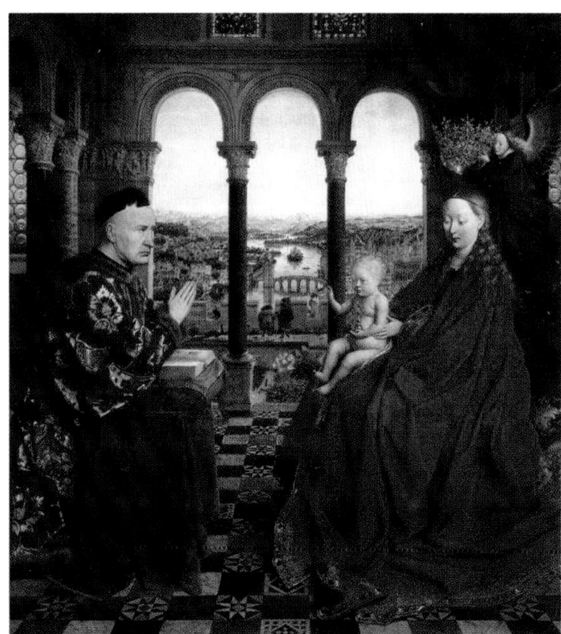

17. Jan van Eyck: The Virgin of Chancellor Rolin (The Louvre, Paris)

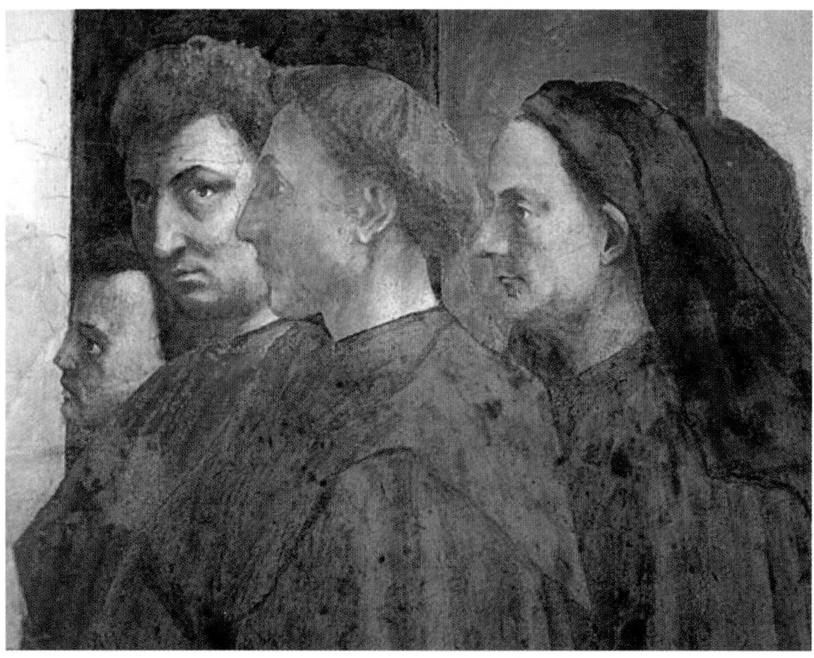

18. Masaccio: Group Portrait of Brunelleschi, Masolino da Panicale, Masaccio himself, and Leon Battista Alberti in The Resurrection of the Son of Theophilos and Saint Peter on a Throne (Brancacci Chapel, Church of Santa Maria del Carmine, Florence)

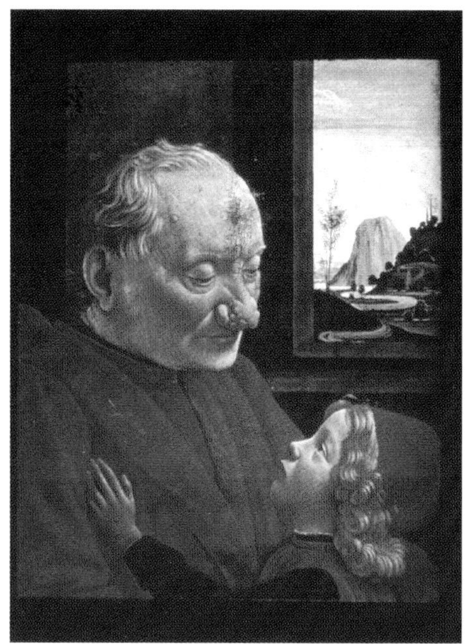

19. Domenico Ghirlandaio: An Old Man and his Grandson (The Louvre, Paris)

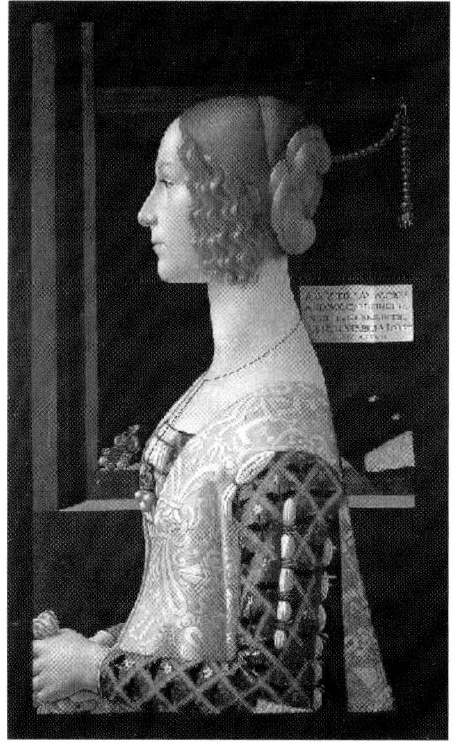

20. Domenico Ghirlandaio: Giovanna Tornabuoni (Thyssen-Bornemisza collection, Lugano-Castagnola, Switzerland)

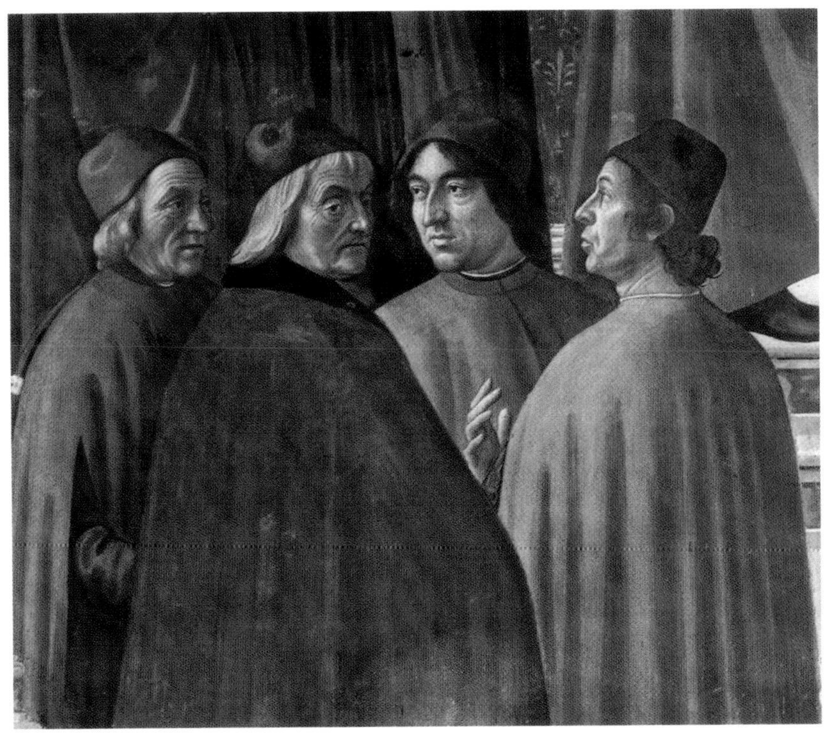

21. Domenico Ghirlandaio: Group portrait from left to right: Marsilio Ficino, Cristoforo Landino, Agnolo Poliziano, and either Demetrio Greco or Gentile de'Becchi in Angel Appearing to Zacharias (Santa Maria Novella Church, Florence)

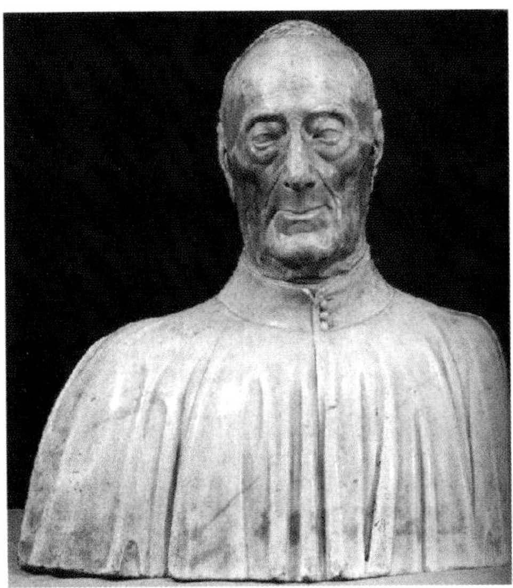

22. Antonio Rossellino: Bust of Giovanni Chellini (Victoria and Albert Museum, London)

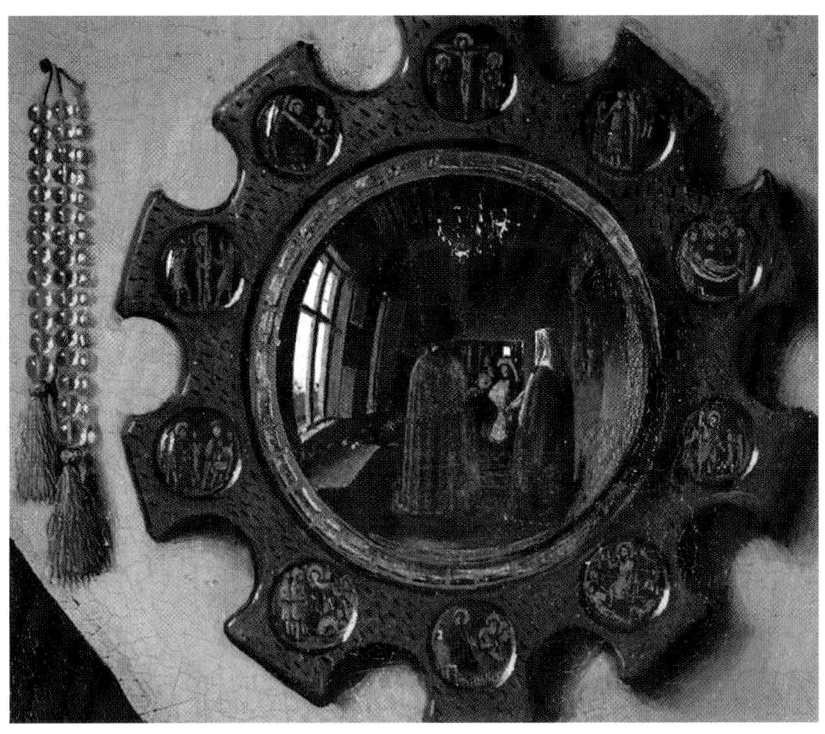

23. Jan van Eyck: Reflections in the Mirror, detail The Betrothal of Giovanni Arnolfini and Jeanne de Chenany (The National Gallery, London)

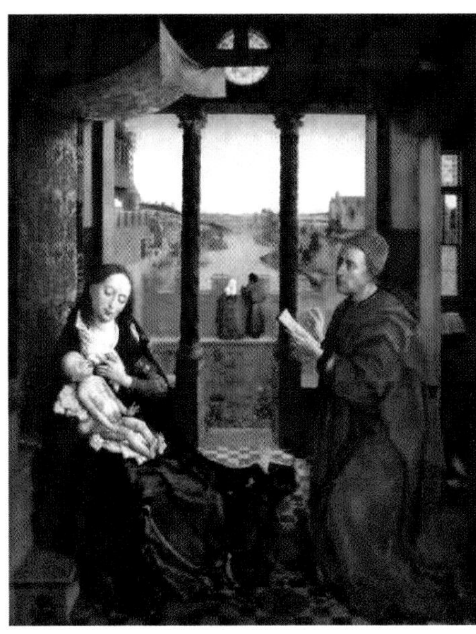

24. Rogier van der Weyden St Luke Painting the Virgin (Museum of Fine Arts, Boston, USA)

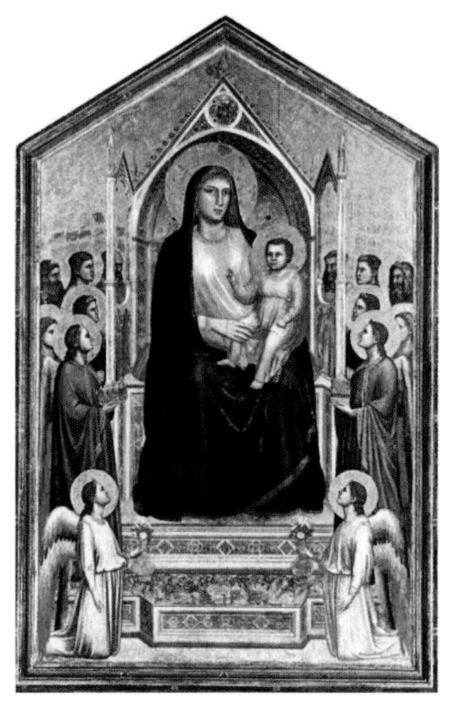

25. *Giotto: Maestà (Uffizi)*

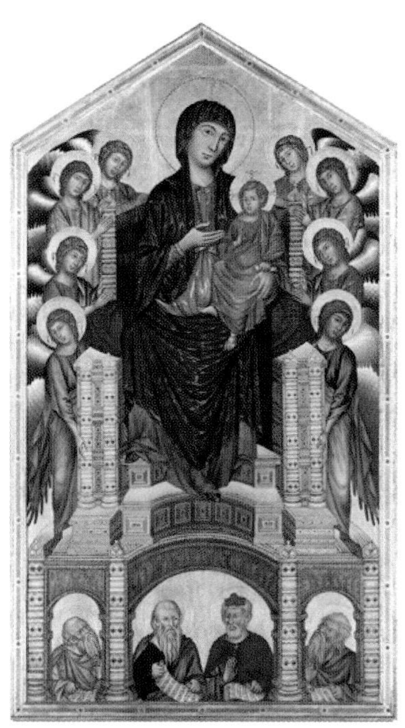

26. *Cimabue: Maestà (Uffizi)*

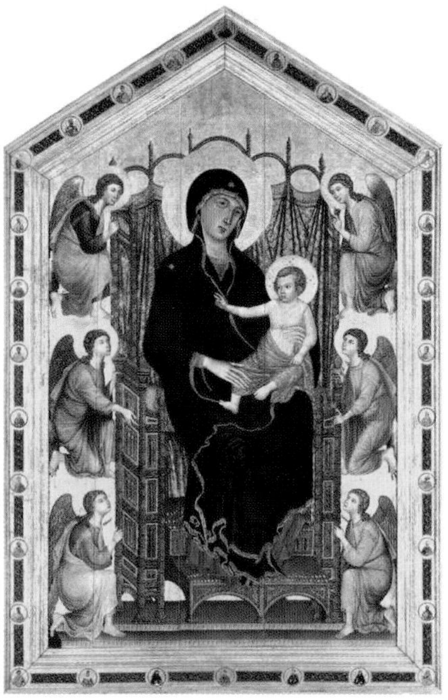

27. *Duccio di Buoninsegna: Maestà (Uffizi)*

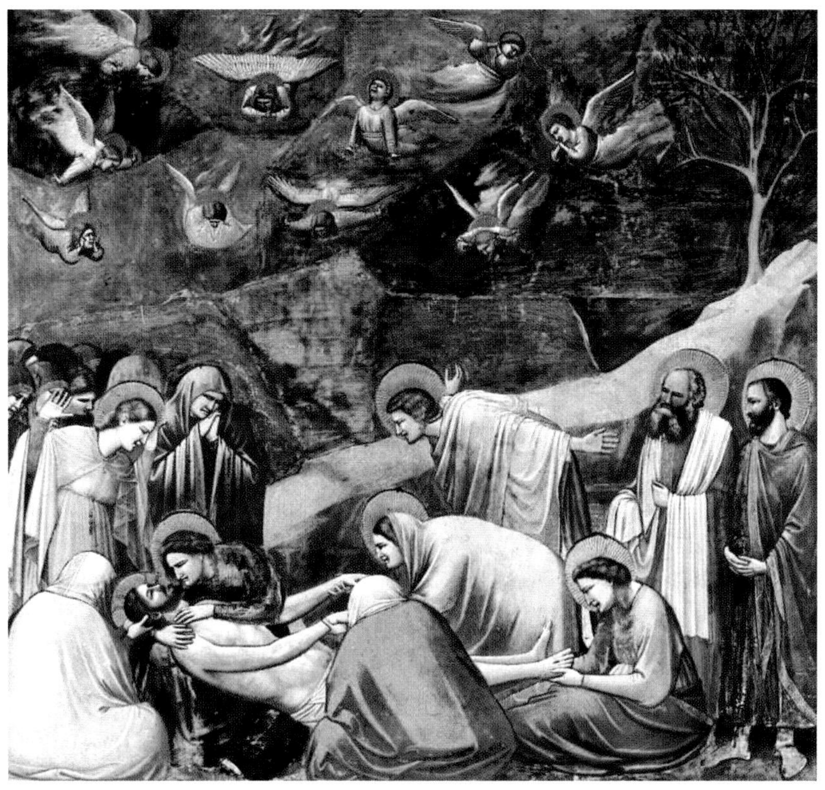

28. Giotto: Lamentation (Arena Chapel, Padua)

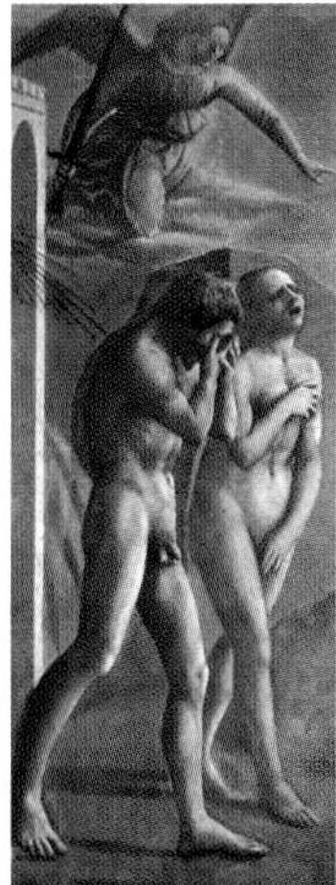

29. Masaccio: Expulsion from Paradise (Brancacci Chapel, Church of Santa Maria del Carmine, Florence)

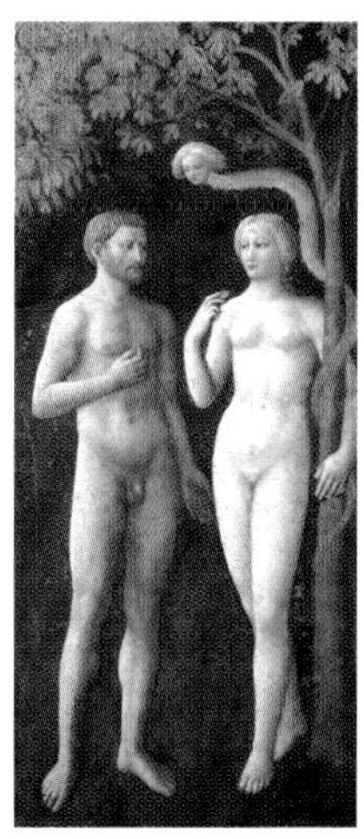

30. Masolino da Panicale: The Temptation (Brancacci Chapel, Church of Santa Maria del Carmine, Florence)

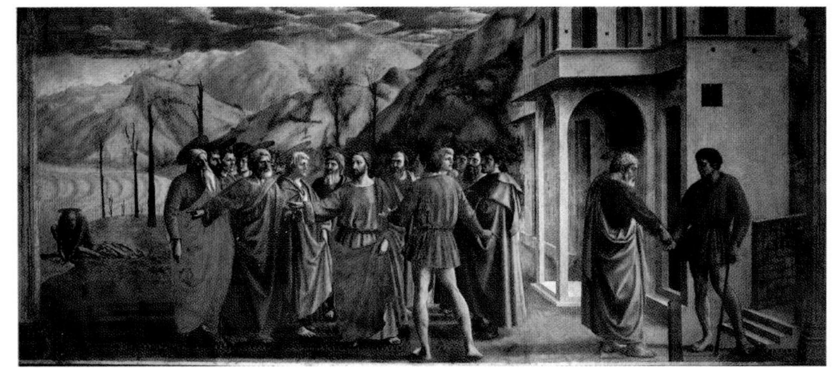

31. Masaccio: The Tribute Money (Brancacci Chapel, Church of Santa Maria del Carmine)

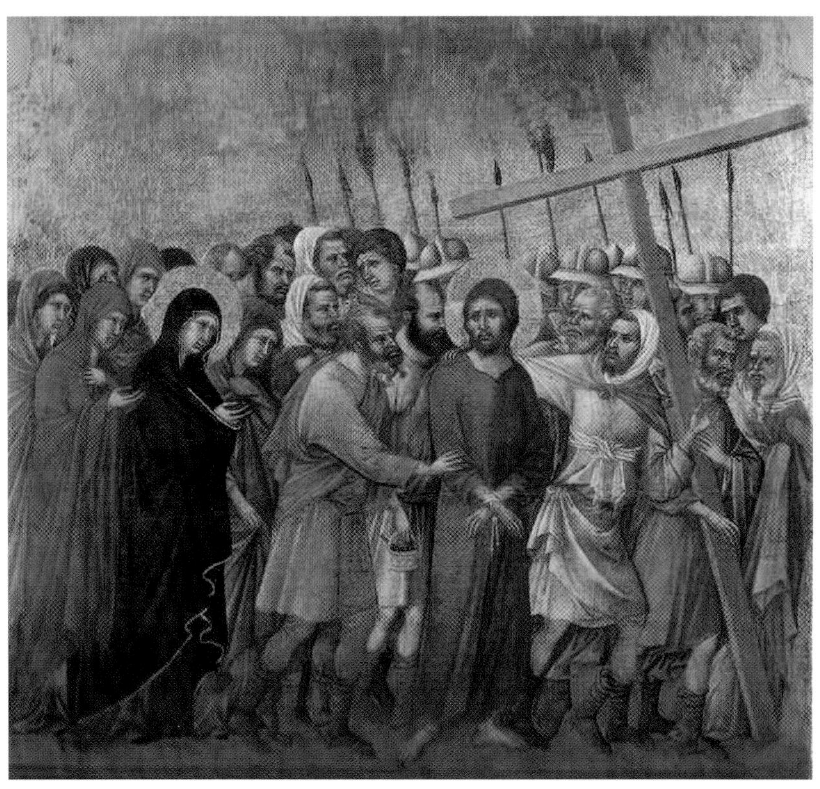

32. Duccio di Buoninsegna: The Way to Calvary (Museo dell'Opera del Duomo, Siena)

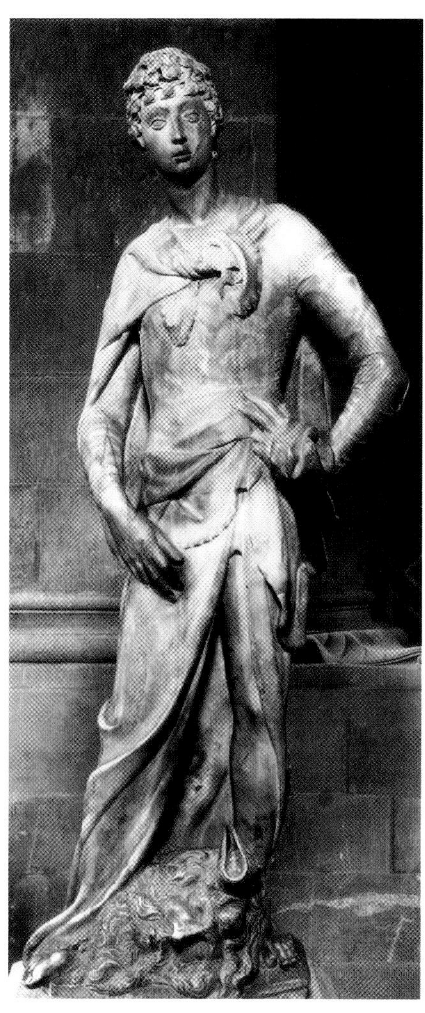

33. Donatello: David, marble (Museo Nazionale del Bargello, Florence)

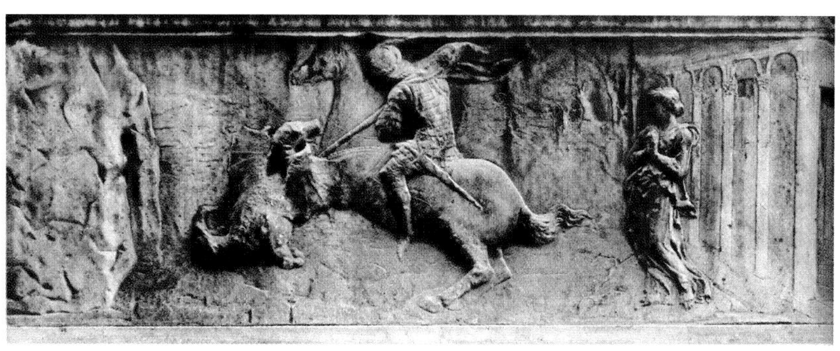

34. Donatello: St George and the Dragon (Orsanmichele, Florence)

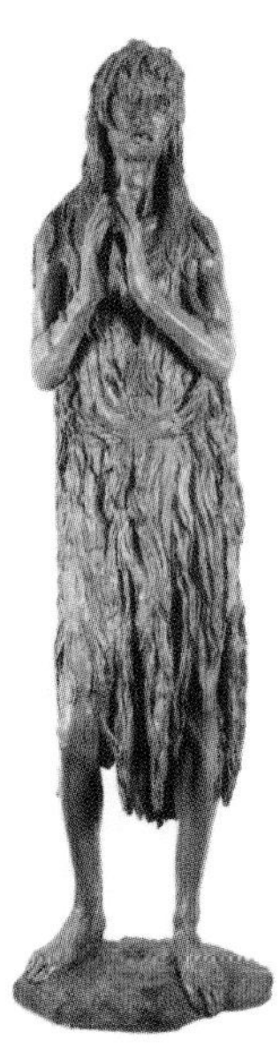

35. Donatello: Penitent Magdalene (Museo dell'Opera del Duomo, Florence)

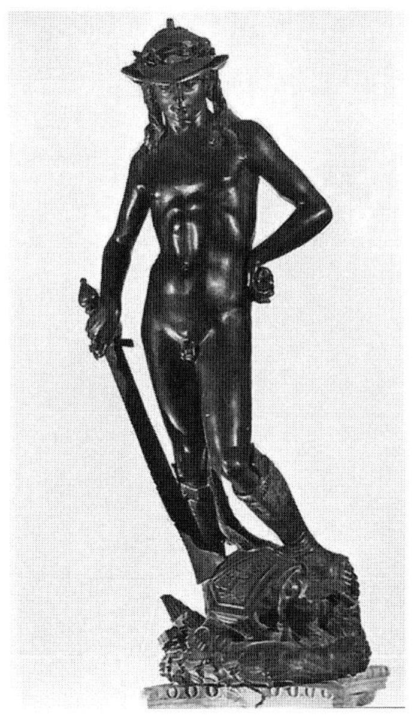

36. Donatello: David, bronze (Museo Nazionale del Bargello, Florence)

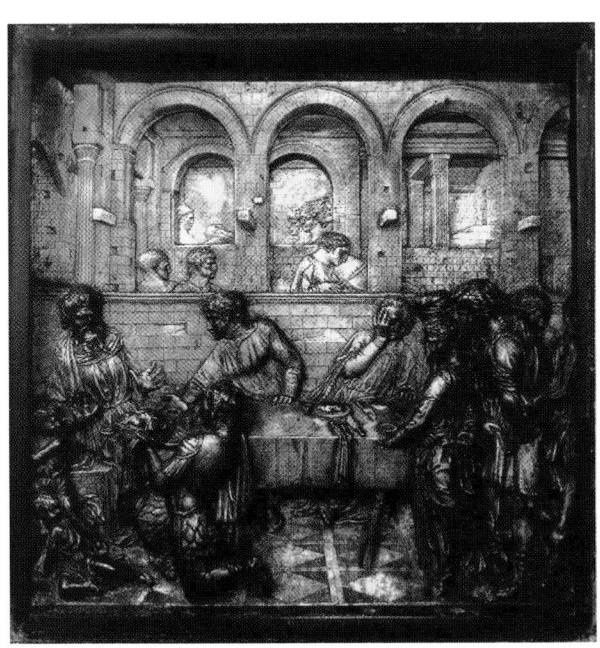

37. Donatello: Feast of Herod (Baptistry Font, Siena)

the microcosm.' Rudolf Arnheim, from whose essay, 'A Review of Proportion' we have just quoted, goes on to state:

> The rationalization of proportion, designed to overcome the uncertainty of intuitive perceptual judgement, suited the demand for scientific exactness, which arose in the Renaissance. It satisfied the yearning for objective description and yielded the rule governing the bewildering complexities of things . . . wherever the scientific ideal and procedure weakened the intuitive powers of the artist or the connoisseur, the crutch of measurement offered to replace the untrustworthy eye.[175]

In his essay entitled *Art and Knowledge*, Joseph Chiari, referring to the sculpture of classical Greece in relation to Italian Renaissance art writes:

> Greek statuary, the product of one of the great moments of man's imagination, has endowed the human body with canons of beauty and harmony that have haunted man's imagination ever since. The notion of beauty, ideal beauty, is Greek, and no other people has contributed more to the revelation of its appearance. After such a dazzling dream, the world seemed to sink back into rest for 15 centuries, before it could again muster the imagination required to give spirit a new impulse and another chance of manifesting itself to man. Dante and Giotto, immortal contemporaries, heralded the rebirth of art, which, after a brief lull in the fourteenth century, burst forth into the greatest flowering of artistic genius the world had ever seen. . . . With Giotto Greek beauty becomes suffused with spiritual naturalness and true humanity, while Fra Angelico, Piero della Francesca, Botticelli, Raphael, da Vinci and Michelangelo render the Divine and the spiritual apprehensible to the senses, through shapes that retain the ideal of Greek beauty but carry with them something that Greek art did not possess, namely the underlying tremor of a deeply felt and an ever-present spiritual life.[176]

9. Sculpture and Architecture

It has already been indicated, on more than one occasion in these pages, that the Italians, in particular the Florentines, believed that art, science and scholarship had flourished in the classical period. They were also of the view that all these things had been destroyed by the northern 'barbarians', the Goths, and that it was up to the Florentines to bring about a renewal of the glorious past and thus bring about a new era.

However, both Ghiberti and Brunelleschi looked beyond the medieval pattern-books to, inter alia, the Campo Santo. Many Pisans had been buried there in Roman sarcophagi, which were richly carved with unclad nymphs representing the human soul, centaurs representing the regions of Hades, and nude human figures in action. Scant though vestiges were, they made clear one of the main differences between classical sculpture and medieval pattern-books: the human figure was generally unclad. In a lecture Rudolf Steiner delivered in Norway on 18 May 1923,[177] he spoke of the difference between the approach of the Greek sculptor and that of the artists of the Renaissance. The Greek sculptors, Steiner maintained, were able to *perceive* the creative activities of the formative life-forces, of the etheric body, in their endeavour to create perfect bodies; they could, in short, perceive the perfect body, though in actual fact, in the external, sense-perceptible physical world, such a body did not exist. By contrast, the Renaissance artists studied anatomy with the thoroughness of the scientists, totally in keeping with the beginning of the age of the consciousness soul.

A significant feature of Ghiberti's second pair of doors is that he breaks with the traditional Byzantine iconography. Instead of no more than two or three figures in a scene there are sometimes upwards of 40, thus reflecting his community spirit.

As we have discussed already, there emerged in the early 1400s an interest in 'humanitas' which contrasted with the formalism of the medieval period. But initially this new interest in Greek and Roman antiquity was restricted to a few scholars, writers and philosophers; at first it did not influence the visual arts. It was in this period that Brunelleschi and Donatello visited Rome. It was, then, in the first decades of the fifteenth century that these two artists set out to create a new attitude to art and to break with the ideas of the past. 'Both were entranced by perspective, by *human nature and by reality as they saw it—not through symbol or myth but directly and clear-sightedly* [my emphasis].'[178] The leader of this group of young Florentine artists was Filippo Brunelleschi (1377–1446). Brunelleschi was employed on the completion of the Gothic Cathedral of Florence. The Florentines wished to have their cathedral crowned by a mighty dome, but no architect had previously been found who had been able to span the immense space between the pillars on which the dome was to rest, till Brunelleschi devised a method of accomplishing this. When he was asked to design new churches or other buildings, he discarded the traditional style altogether and adopted the programme of those in Florence who longed for a revival of classical grandeur. What he achieved was the creation of a new way of building, in which the forms of classical architecture were freely used to create new modes of *beauty and harmony*. Brunelleschi succeeded in making his programme come true. For nearly 500 years the architects of Europe and America followed in his footsteps. Wherever we go in cities and villages we find buildings in which classical forms, such as columns or pediments are used. It is true that, in the twentieth century architects began to veer away from the Renaissance tradition—just as Brunelleschi had revolted against the Gothic tradition. However, even today, many houses that are being built, even those with no columns or similar trimmings, still, to a greater or lesser extent, preserve remnants of classical form in the shape of mouldings on doors and window frames, or in the measurements and proportions of the buildings. As Gombrich expresses it: 'If Brunelleschi wanted to create the architecture of a new era, he certainly succeeded.'[179] His buildings mark the start of Renaissance architecture.

Gothic style churches had become the normal settings for prayer and liturgy in Italy since the late twelfth century. The principles introduced c.1421 by Brunelleschi in his design of San Lorenzo in Florence were both bold and novel. Interior spaces were not 'rushed up' in shafts and dissipated in lofty arched roofs. Such spaces were to be created through rows of columns and pilasters ruled across by continuous bands of moulding and, through the use of a single measurement, that determined through a system of ratios the relationships between nave columns and aisle chapels, the breadth and height occupied by both. The sense of an enclosed space, in which man without distractions, could find peace within himself, was enhanced by a flat, boxing-in ceiling to the nave. In contrast to the Gothic, decorative features were to be reticent. Capitals were to be identical rather than eye-catchingly decorative. Architectural sculpture—statuary in porches, sprouting from ribs and arches, and so forth, were no longer included in the overall structure. 'The aim of the new canon of beauty was clarification and lucidity.'[180] (Plate 4 San Lorenzo Church.) Working on a much smaller scale in his design some ten years later Brunelleschi designed the Pazzi Chapel for the powerful family of the Pazzi in the cloister of another Florentine church, Santa Croce. Plate 5 shows the façade of this little chapel. We see that it has little in common with any classical temple; and even less with the forms used by the Gothic builders. Brunelleschi has combined columns, pilasters and arches in his own way to achieve an effect of lightness and grace which is different from anything that preceded it. Moreover, the portico (built after Brunelleschi's death but corresponding to his design) serves to 'filter' the light coming in from outside. In this way the light admitted by the entrance wall merges with the light from the dome, the light from heaven, creating a uniform illumination. Details such as the framing of the portico door, with its classical gable or pediment, show that Brunelleschi had studied such an ancient building as the Pantheon. Compare how the arch is formed and how it 'cuts into' the upper storey with its pilasters. We recognize Roman forms even more clearly as we enter the chapel. Nothing in this bright and well-proportioned interior has any of the features characteristic of Gothic architecture. There are no high windows, no pillars. Instead the blank white wall is subdivided by grey pilasters, which convey the idea of a classical 'order', although they serve no real function in the construction of the building.[181]

Though no record exists that the Pazzi Chapel became for architects what Masaccio's Brancacci Chapel frescoes became for painters, Brunelleschi's simplicity, clarity and calmly calculated mode of design resonated on through the work of Florentines who grew up with them as, for instance, Michelangelo did. For example, the spare and luminous space Andrea Palladio (1508–80) created from rows of columns below and rounded voids and solids above echoed the intention of the early Florentine post-Gothic: to enlist, as it were, mathematics and geometry in the service of worship is beautifully manifest in the Redentore Church, Venice (Plate 6).

Brunelleschi's first architectural commission was the Foundling Hospital, the *Ospedale degli Innocenti* (1419–c.1445). *Ospedale degli Innocenti* was the first institution of its kind in Europe. It was created to take care of and bring up orphans and abandoned children as well as give them a trade.[182] Florence's citizen-supported hospitals were a source of pride to the Renaissance city, and her system of lay fraternities and their charitable activities is a unique aspect of the city's sense of *civitas*. In providing a suitable home for one of these caretaking institutions, Brunelleschi's

Ospedale degli Innocenti, 'brings in effect the architectural language of the monastic cloister, with its ordered rhythm of arcades, to the public square. Monasteries were often the sole refuge of orphans. Brunelleschi therefore brought not only the physical form of the cloister but its association to the *res publica* [the general public good or welfare].'[183] The façade of this complex to house orphans uses slender columns to support round arches and a simple horizontal entablature. The cornice serves as a base for a row of windows with classically-inspired pediments, one centred above each arch. The distance between the columns is the same as the distance from the columns to the back wall of the arcade. The distance between the floor of the loggia to just above the impost blocks is also the same. Thus the cube is a major module in this proportional design. Other geometrical relationships governed the location of the cornice, the widths of the doors and heights of the window (Plate 7).

Guglielmo Amerighi in his introductory book *The City of Florence* observes that no more than 50 years after the formation of the Gothic city, the features of Florence were profoundly changed by a far-reaching modification in architecture. The change was due to Filippo Brunelleschi:

> The imprint he left on the city was so important in itself and in its consequences that we might truly say that he founded a new Florence . . . Now let us see what happened in Florence between 1420 and 1440. Brunelleschi built the Old Sacristy of San Lorenzo, the Pazzi Chapel, the Colonnade of the Foundling Hospital, San Lorenzo, Santo Spirito, the Great Cloister of Santa Croce, and the cupola and lantern of the Cathedral. And with this the architectural face of the western world changed.[184]

Donatello seemed to have been particularly impressed by the realism of Roman portrait sculpture, for on his return to Florence he sculpted for the west façade of Giotto's campanile, a statue of a prophet, modelling it closely on one of his friends. The *Zuccone (Habakkuk)*, (c.1427–36) as it is called, depicts an aged man with blear eyes, cavernous mouth and sloping arms. It is a work of uncompromising realism. Vasari relates that Donatello, while completing the final delicate touches would repeatedly mutter, 'Speak, damn you, speak!' What Donatello achieved here was the representation of an individual male, with certain characteristic features, which rendered him quite other than any other human being. Vasari's claim reflects the age-old praise that only a lack of breath distinguishes a stone figure from the living, and is both a tribute to the compelling power of the statue and a recognition of Donatello's creative greatness.

The head of the *Jeremiah* (c.1423–5), also sculpted for Giotto's campanile, has the same sense of *individuality* as that of the *Zuccone (Habakkuk)*. (Plates 8 and 9.) From the 1430s onwards Donatello's large sculpture completely breaks with tradition and is more or less free-standing. To the modern mind a free-standing figure in the round, such as Donatello's bronze *David* (c.1446–c.1460), seems quite natural, makes little impression, since the type of the person standing in his or her individual space, separate from anyone else, is so much part of the modern experience, of the experience of objective self-consciousness (consciousness soul).

In the area of sculpture, it was in Italy that we can perceive the most radical departure from its heritage (just it had done in the area of architecture). This achievement was intimately bound up with another: the 'discovery' of the human body and of how man lives 'within' his limbs. What we see expressed here is man's 'stepping out' of a group-like self-awareness into an evolving self-contained consciousness, a consciousness of self, freed from the bonds which still prevailed and found expression in, say, the architectural sculpture of a Gothic cathedral such as Chartres.[185] In a lecture he gave, entitled in English 'From Space Perspective to Colour Perspective', Rudolf Steiner makes a statement in which he expresses man's relation to space since the beginning of the fifteenth century in the following way: 'In sculpture man's soul wishes to sculpt the kind of statue in which man [i.e. each individual person] is given a meaningful place in space ... according to his nature.'[186] On numerous occasions Steiner points out that from the early fifteenth century it was man's task to begin to develop the seed of his own egohood, so that standing alone in freedom, he could make free decisions. Margaret Bennell, in her *Shakespeare's Flowering of the Spirit* writes: 'A thoughtful study of history reveals this gradual change, which even yet is not complete, from men and women living entirely within the life-stream of their tribe or family, to men and women beginning to free themselves from the blood-tie and to stand alone, supported by their own inner forces in the place of group custom and convention.'[187]

10. Brunelleschi and Alberti

> Perspective is the rein and rudder of painting.
>
> *(Leonardo da Vinci)*

Brunelleschi's handling of the problem of space in the many buildings he designed and executed led him to develop a more exact manner of rendering space on a two-dimensional surface.[188] Up until then the artist's understanding of perspective devices had been tentative, and interiors, for example, were often distorted, elongated, or set at an angle in order to fit in all the many elements of activity relevant to the scene depicted. Brunelleschi, as both an architect and a sculptor must have needed sketches and designs to illustrate his projects and realized that it was difficult, if not impossible, to give a realistic effect of distance, of spatial proportions, without a consistent system of perspective. Eventually what Brunelleschi achieved was a system of perspective with mathematical, regular diminution towards a fixed vanishing point.

In 1435 the young Leon Battista Alberti (1404–1474) wrote a book on painting in Latin. The next year he rewrote it in Italian (*Della Pittura*) and dedicated it to Brunelleschi. For more than one reason it was the most influential of all the early Renaissance treatises on art. Alberti's treatise on painting, usually referred to as the *Della Pittura*, sounded the reveille of modern times and modern thought. This finds expression in, for instance, his explicit assumption that picture-making meant the depiction of human figures in action and with movements and gestures corresponding to psychological and emotional states. In one place Alberti refers to 'we painters who wish to show the movements of the soul by means of the movements of the limbs'. A few lines before this he says:

> It is, therefore, necessary that painters should have command over all the movements of the body, which they will learn well, from nature, in order to imitate the many movements of the soul, even though this is difficult. Who, without trying it, would believe how difficult it is to depict a laughing face without making it appear sorrowful rather than joyous? And, in the same way, who without much study, can draw faces in which the chin, eyes, cheeks, and forehead, all unite in laughing or weeping at the same time? To do this it is necessary to *learn*

> *from nature* [my emphasis] and always to seek after the most fugitive aspects of things. . . .[189]

This treatise on painting included a discussion of the laws of mathematical perspective for artists. This gave perspective a scientific basis and made spatial measurement accurate for the first time. As Brunelleschi made no written record of his perspective findings, it remained for Alberti to be the *first* to put the theory into writing. Such a discovery was clearly of great significance. The exact representation of three dimensional space had been beyond the capability of medieval painters. *Objects*, both animate and inanimate, *exist in space. Man's relation to physical space, therefore, took on a new dimension—beginning in the first half of the fifteenth century.*

Mortimer Wheeler, discussing Roman landscape painting and relief sculpture (for example, Trajan's Column) in connection with perspective, makes the following statement:

> The strange failure of classical art to work out the mechanism of perspective, even when, as under the early Empire, the time was aesthetically ripe for it, no doubt helped a little to impede the further development of landscape as a mode in its own right. This failure is more remarkable in that as far back as the fifth century BC the mathematical ingenuity of the Greek mind had nearly solved the problem.[190]

Alberti also described how an artist could obtain a correct view of a scene by observing it through a thin veil, or *velo*. The idea is that we can get a correct image of an object viewed through such a veil or 'window' by tracing the outline of it on the 'window' glass. Albrecht Dürer designed several such apparatuses. The earliest surviving use of linear perspective in art is attributed to Donato de Bardi (1386–1466), known as Donatello. We see that it was early in the age of the objective self-consciousness (the consciousness soul) that linear perspective was 'invented'. This is a typical aspect of modern consciousness that wishes to paint pictures exactly as the eye sees them, and to achieve this aim consciously creates an optical illusion. In the lecture by Rudolf Steiner on perspective already referred to he said 'it was essential to mankind's evolution to conjure spatial perspective on to a flat surface, and it had to come'. He then went on to state: 'But it has to be surmounted. Not that in the future we need not understand perspective. We must understand it, yet we must be capable of returning to colour perspective, and make use of it again.'

In this connection it is of interest to quote a few words from the studies of modern art by the German art historian Werner Hofmann. He reminds us that it was early in the twentieth century that purely abstract painting made its appearance. Kandinsky, for example, was among the first to paint completely non-figurative compositions consisting only of colours, lines and shapes. In the other arts, including music, similar decisive changes occur. Referring to the art of painting Hofmann characterized the transition as follows:

> In 1910 the development of modern art reached its turning point . . . the historical construction proved itself to be superficial and exhausted, mere props of a larger, many-layered reality. The ideas behind the objects demanded recognition. A Platonic philosophy cleared the way for appearance into the zones of reality. In the artistic camps the process of making the invisible visible was felt as a gain of new levels of experience. It was also felt as a manifestation of a vitality hitherto hidden in artistic means and techniques. These decades not only penetrated unexplored levels of reality, but also worked more and more consciously at a full understanding of its formal and chromatic vocabulary. . . . The step achieved by Kandinsky in 1910 was intended to free artistic expression for the task of addressing the *how*, for coming to grips with its spiritual mandate, and to bring into the clear light of day an art pure and eternal, freed from the burden of everything of a physical, material nature.[191]

All through medieval times attempts at perspective, the science of simulation of space on a flat surface, had been intuitive rather than scientific. Giotto developed a kind of empirical perspective, but it was Masaccio who, with the assistance of his contemporaries Brunelleschi and Donatello, was the first painter who represented human figures and inanimate objects in space on the foundation of a scientifically established method of perspective. But now a 'scientific' method was established. In 1435, Leon Battista Alberti (1404–72), in his seminal book *De Pictura* (1435), the first version of *On Painting*, translated by him into Italian under the title *Della Pittura* in 1436, the rules were laid out clearly and scientifically. It was a 'man-made' solution, to illustrate from the individual's point of view of which he is 'centre and measure'.

It was not only painters and sculptors but also writers who were beginning to 'speak' of the world, not how it looks absolutely, but how it looks to *them, individually*; not how things are in the sight of God, but how things appeared to them, from their angle, at a particular point in time. Don Cupitt in *After God, The Future of Religion* writes:

> The reason [Jan] van Eyck's old faces are so remarkably intense and memorable is that he really does want to teach us to see the world and one another from a finite, human, and mortal point of view. I think he would like to convince us ... that the individual mortal human's perception of his mortal fellow human, in its very transience, can somehow be more real and more *detailed* than the old grand public and theological vision.[192]

Another name by which one-point, or centralized, perspective is known is artificial perspective, because it was not a given part of nature itself, but the creation of the human mind. 'What we see here is that the study of nature was becoming a science.'[193]

A telling example of how useful one-point perspective could be to the artist for portraying space is Donatello's panel of the *Dance of Salome* (c.1425). We shall look at this panel more closely when we come to discuss Donatello's sculptural work in more detail. Science and art were 'intermingled', as it were, in the Italian Renaissance, with artists such as Leonardo da Vinci making observational drawings of anatomy and nature. Yet, as J. Brotton reminds us,[194] the most significant development of the era was not a specific discovery, but rather a *process* for discovery, *the scientific method.* This new way of learning about the world—and the human being—focused on empirical evidence, the importance of mathematics, and discarded the Aristotelian 'final cause' in favour of a mechanical philosophy. The new scientific method led to great contributions not only in the field of anatomy but also in those of astronomy, physics and biology.[195]

Gerardus van der Leeuw, in his fascinating work *Sacred and Profane Beauty, The Holy in Art*, refers to a study by the German psychologist H.G. Evers, who stated that drawing in perspective means a change in the way man is situated in the world, to which he no longer belongs as one component among others but, rather, stands in contrast to it, *as an ego*, freed from it.[196] With linear perspective the fifteenth century Florentines not only had a method to render a scene in correct perspective, recreating almost exactly what the eye saw, but they also felt that the key had been found which could unlock the divine order of the cosmos. Since at least the time of Pythagoras[197] in ancient Greece, people had believed that the universe was ordered in accord with sacred numerical relationships and proportions, by *sacred geometry.* No wonder that painters, sculptors and architects of the Renaissance could claim that man as a creative being was capable of achieving divinity (see chapters 5 and 8), for here they could experience and vicariously participate in the very process of the mathematical creation of the universe through the recreation of 'worlds' of harmony in their own works. The development of linear perspective brought a new worldview into being. Most obvious is a sense of being completely *at home in the world and an integral part of it*—'quite different', Susan Fegley Osmond emphasizes, 'from the medieval feeling of being stranded in a realm of mortality while one's true habitat is some great dimensionless beyond.'[198] Earlier attempts at perspective—by Giotto, for example—revealed man *descending to earth*, as it were, but with linear perspective he really *landed*—and not only in the realm of painting. Medieval painting—we may think here of Russian or Greek religious icons—had no extension in depth and no horizon.

> Renaissance man discovered extension, then discovered the horizon—and then wanted to extend his horizons! ... with the help of the geometry through which artist-architect had first made a graph of space, explorers eventually found a way to graph their way across trackless seas.... Now seeming to be set on a course to fulfil the biblical dictum to become the lord of creation Renaissance man set out the world's territory, and likewise to master the workings of the universe through science.... The post-medieval Western mind seeks to find underlying laws and principles and to form an understanding of how they interrelate so as to make a grid or framework upon which all knowledge can be plotted and connected and formed into a solid edifice.[199]

Linear perspective implies the quest for *objectivity* in knowledge. In viewing the world as though through a window, early Renaissance man, artists, mentally set themselves apart from their subjects—they became *observers* from outside a literal frame of reference. They then set about attempting to record everything within that frame as exactly as possible—without preconception. 'Yet', Osmond rightly states,

> Perspective also manifests the subjectivity of knowledge. What you see in your frame of reference changes depending on your position. This yields a certain angle that obstructs certain elements while it reveals others. Your perception of reality is inevitably slanted and your knowledge limited. *It is also uniquely your own* [my emphasis].[200]

We could say that, in this context, linear perspective endows unique power to the *individual observer*. The individual becomes the main arbiter of his perceptions and of his relationship to the world. Another significant point we may bear in mind is that linear perspective also ran parallel with, gave 'support' to, the changing understanding of the relationship between man and God during the Renaissance.

Medieval depictions had no point of infinity such as that implied in linear perspective's vanishing point. Father God, the infinitely supernal, was conceived as some divine omnipotence way beyond the heavens. Linear perspective's vanishing point brought the infinite 'down', as it were, into the finite, the phenomenal world. Linear perspective circumscribes the world so that we are 'cut off' from the magical—'that "spaceless" space in medieval art from which objects seem to appear and disappear' (Osmond). But, as we have just seen, linear perspective opens a previously unknown window. In religious art it is a window, as Erwin Panofsky expresses it, 'onto the realm of the visionary, where the miraculous becomes a direct experience of the beholder, in that the supernatural events in a sense erupt into his own, apparently natural visual space and so permit him really to "internalize" their supernaturalness'.[201]

It was in painting where the new ways of man experiencing himself and his possibilities first found expression—in particular, in Florence—in the art and science of perspective. This science, prefiguring the spatial discoveries of explorers such as Christopher Columbus (1451–1506) who, in 1498, discovered the mainland of South America, and the Portuguese Vasco da Gama (c.1469–1524), perfected a method of conveying an impression of spatial extension in depth. John Lane finds a felicitous and pertinent mode of expression here:

> The interest in depth, in itself symptomatic of a new interest in externalities, was only one of a number of radical new elements—amongst them, a single viewpoint, an analytical approach, and a concern for the representation of the visible world on a flat surface—which were aspects of the changed, or rather changing, world-view.[202]

The researches of Brunelleschi, Alberti, and Piero della Francesca replaced medieval attitudes with a method based on a point of view both unique and rational—the point of view of a single, detached observer.

It is in the paintings of Piero della Francesca (1416–92) that the Florentine preoccupation not only with the rendering of physical reality and space, but also movement and immediacy in storytelling, found a harmonious and definite solution. Rosa Maria Letts, in her book, *The Renaissance*, says that Piero della Francesca's *Maria della Misericordia* (c.1462), makes us realize that Brunelleschi's focused system of perspective, and:

> Masaccio's volumes and Donatello's realism had not been in vain. They had found their true synthesis in the effortless realism of Piero's art. The round golden arch of the frame echoes the Virgin's cloak as it opens like a dome to receive the believer. She appears more than real, more than present.... In her perfect symmetry, her timeless features and forms, the Virgin shelters and protects the believer.... It is as if, like the dome of Florence's cathedral, she could embrace all people. This new reality of Piero della Francesca has no doubts; it needs no verification; it just exists.[203] [Plate 10.]

The artist and art historian Dorothea Blom comments in regard to the Florentine use of the laws of geometrical perspective:

> The Florentine passion for measuring in the fifteenth century paved the way for responding to reality, secular and religious, in terms of measurements and the three dimensional, a very radical way of seeing at the time. By the nineteenth century, this way of seeing had become academic and stale.... The art of today is obviously not a mere pictorial record of ancient events.[204] [See Werner Hofmann's statement re Kandinsky above.]

Albrecht Dürer (1471–1528) considered himself to be a pupil of the Italian Renaissance and to be its missionary. In his theoretical books he strove to explain to his German readers how the new conception of art differed fundamentally from the one with which they were familiar. He insisted that there were good, and rational, grounds on which the traditional methods of German Gothic painting could be criticized.

> Up to now many able boys in our German lands were placed with painters to learn the art, where, however, they were taught without any rational principle and solely according to current usage. And thus they grew up in ignorance, like a wild and unpruned tree. True it is, that some of them acquired a ready hand by steady practice, so that their work was produced powerfully, but without forethought and simply as it pleased them. Whenever knowledgeable painters and true masters saw such unconsidered work, they laughed at the blindness of these people, and not unfairly so, since nothing is less pleasing to a man of good sense than mistakes in painting, however much diligence may have been employed in the work. But the fact that such painters were

> pleased by their own errors is only due to their never having learned the skill of measurement, without which nobody can become a proper workman.[205]

Trained in the tradition of the workshop run by Michael Wolgemut (1434–1519), painter, woodcarver and engraver, Dürer himself must have experienced the shock of discovering that there were so many shortcomings, mistakes, in that school once the significance of perspective, of being able to conjure up, for instance, a convincing and physically realistic interior, had been brought home; and once Italian engravings, notably those of Andrea Mantegna (1431–1506), had revealed to him the character of a correctly structured nude. That 'measurement', mathematics, could serve to eliminate mistakes in perspective presented no problem to Dürer; the problem of the rendering of the nude human body was more elusive. It was clearly not just accuracy that was needed. The Italians, Dürer realized, seemed to possess another secret, the secret of beauty. 'Nothing is more moving in Dürer's writings', Gombrich claims, 'than his struggle with this enigmatic problem'.[206]

Alberti regarded mathematics as the common ground of art and science. In both *Della Pittura* and *De Statua*, a short treatise on sculpture, Alberti stressed that 'all steps of learning should be learnt from nature'. The ultimate aim of an artist is to imitate nature. Painters and sculptors strive 'as nearly as possible that the work they have undertaken shall appear to the observer to be similar to the real objects of nature'. However, Alberti clearly did not mean that artists should imitate nature objectively, as it is, but the artist should be especially attentive to *beauty*, 'for in painting beauty is as pleasing as it is necessary'. A true work of art is, according to Alberti, so constructed that it is impossible to take anything away from it or add anything to it, without impairing the beauty of the whole. Beauty was for Alberti 'the harmony of all parts in relation to one another'; this concord is realized in a particular number, proportion, and arrangement demanded by harmony. Alberti's thoughts on harmony were not new, for they could be traced back to Pythagoras, but he set them in a fresh context, which well fitted in with contemporary aesthetic thinking.[207]

With the discovery of the classical Roman modes of architecture, a gradual transition can be seen in the fifteenth century in Italy in the plans of churches from the traditional Latin cross to the centralized form. Centralized churches posed the problem of the hierarchical separation of clergy and congregation, and, in particular, it raised the question as to the site of the altar. However, the subtle qualities of centralized geometry were irresistible. A key work in the understanding of this geometry was the architectural treatise *De Aedificatoria*, written between 1443 and 1452 by Alberti. The pre-Christian origins of his ideas are shown very clearly in his designs for temples, as he called churches. Of the nine forms he uses, the circle is the primary one.[208] Alberti was inspired by Vitruvian buildings of the classical era, but, strangely, the central form which he favoured was not common in temples of that period.[209] Indeed, Vitruvius did not even include round buildings among the seven classes of temple he enumerated.

In Renaissance plans of a centralized church each part is related harmonically to the other parts, like the members of a human body, making manifest the nature of divinity. The church is designed as a visible manifestation of the divine harmony—in essence a Neoplatonic concept. It was to be covered by a fine dome. 'The vault of the dome was to bear a likeness of the sky, in the tradition of the universal cosmic interpretation of the temple. Thus, as in eastern Orthodox architecture . . . the whole round church was emblematical of the world—the created manifestation of the Word of God: a perfect vessel for humanity. Like the round churches of the Templar period,[210] such central churches were seen not only as microcosms of the world, but also as symbolic of the universality of God.'[211]

Rudolf Steiner, in a lecture entitled 'The Relationship of Man with the Cosmos', speaks in some detail regarding this relationship. One statement runs: 'The human form is a most marvellous structure. Think, to begin with, of the *head*. In all its parts, the head is a copy of the universe. Its form is spherical, the spherical form being modified at the base in order to provide for the articulation of other organs and systems. The essential form of the head, however, is a copy of the spherical form of the universe.'[212]

Ficino regarded God as the true centre of the universe, the inner core of everything, but at the same time as the circumference of the universe. The geometrical definition of God through the symbol of the circle or sphere has a pedigree reaching back to the Orphic poets. It was vitalized by Plato and made the central notion of his cosmological myth in the *Timaeus*. It was given pre-eminence in the works of Plotinus and, dependent on him, in the writings of the pseudo-Dionysius the Areopagite which were followed by the mystical theologians of the Middle Ages.

Renaissance architects, as their various treatises show, were steeped in the ideas which, with the surge of Platonism and Neoplatonism in the fifteenth century, had spread quickly. The fundamental principle of the correspondence of microcosm and macrocosm is an ancient Greek schema of seeing the same patterns occurring in all levels of existence. It may have been first recognized by Democritus in the fifth century BC or with Pythagoras and is a philosophical conception which runs through Socrates and Plato and acquired new life in the Renaissance. This conception, together with the harmonic structure of the universe, also emanating from Greece, and the comprehension of God through the geometrical symbols of centre, circle, and sphere—all these closely related ideas which had roots in antiquity found visual expression in the Renaissance church.[213] For the perceptive man of the Renaissance this church architecture with its strict geometry, the equipoise of its harmonic order, and above all, with the sphere of the dome, echoed and at the same time revealed the perfection, truth and omnipotence of God. Wittkower observes that the realization of these ideas in the Renaissance church:

> . . . betrays by implication a shift in the religious feeling itself, a shift for which the change from the basilica to the centralized church is a more telling symbol than the changes in the philosophical interpretation of God and world. . . . The builders of the Middle Ages laid out their churches *in modum crucis*—their Latin Cross plan was the symbolic expression of Christ crucified. The Renaissance . . . did not lose sight of this idea. What had changed was the conception of the godhead: Christ as the essence of perfection and harmony superseded Him who had suffered on the Cross for humanity; the Pantocrator replaced the Man of Sorrows.[214]

Circular churches, however, enjoyed only a short-lived success. Most of them were constructed in the years 1490–1560. The ancient proportions were so closely allied with pre-Christian religion, that it was only a matter of time before the Church rejected Alberti's circular 'temples' on the grounds of their pagan origin. However, the overall system, related to the ideal proportions of Vitruvian Man was considered admirable when applied to the orthodox-shaped churches of the Renaissance.[215] Nevertheless, the fundamental principle of the correspondence of microcosm and macrocosm was not recognized by the Church and was rejected by Rome. It is beyond the scope of these pages to substantiate why Rudolf Steiner emphasized that this principle should again be recognized. Here we shall merely quote two relevant sentences from the many statements he made in this connection. On one occasion he stated: 'Processes which take place within the human being must correspond with processes in the universe outside. We must be able to find the outer processes corresponding to every inner process.'[216]

> Man is born from the whole cosmos. He must look up to it as to his father–mother being of whom he himself is an image. Yes, man is an image of the whole world with which he is acquainted. There is nothing in the being of man that does not in some way relate to what can be found in the great cosmos.[217]

All that can said here in connection with Steiner's conception of the relationship between man, the microcosm, and the universe, the macrocosm, is that it is far more comprehensive than that propounded by the Greeks and the Italians of the Renaissance period.

11. Renaissance Experience of the Natural World, of Open and Enclosed Space

Attention has already been drawn to the fact that at the Florentine Platonic Academy scant attention was paid to the Aristotelian stream, that, in other words, scientific investigation in the strictest sense was not undertaken. 'But', as Jacob Burckhardt claims in *The Civilization of the Renaissance in Italy*, 'outside the sphere of scientific investigation, there is another way to draw near to nature. The Italians are the first among modern peoples by whom the outward world was seen and felt as something beautiful.'[218] To the Italian in the fourteenth and fifteenth centuries nature had lost its taint of sin. It was St Francis of Assisi (c.1181–1226) who had given birth, as it were, to such a feeling for and understanding of nature, for in *The Canticle of Brother Sun*, later to be called *The Canticle of the Creatures*, he praises the Lord for creating the heavenly bodies, the four elements and 'Sister Earth, our mother /Who feeds us in her sovereignty and produces/ Various fruit with coloured flowers and herbs.' (*Laudat si, mi Signore, per sora nostra matre Terra, / la quale ne sustenta e governa / e produce diversa fructi con coloriti fiori et herba.*)[219]

But the clear proofs of a deepening effect of the beauty and richness of nature on the human spirit manifest themselves in the writings of Dante and Petrarch. It is in the latter's work that the significance of nature for a receptive spirit is clearly displayed. Landscape, it is clear, is one of the principal means by which artists express their delight in the visible world.[220] In the fifteenth century it was first the great masters of the Flemish school, the brothers van Eyck,[221] who observed nature in remarkable detail. Their landscapes are truly beautiful. They are, moreover, not merely the result of an endeavour to reflect the real world in art, but also have a certain poetical meaning—in short, a soul. Their influence on the whole art of the west is apparent, and extended to the landscape painting of the Italians. In increasing measure during the fifteenth century interest in the natural world, the visible material world, grew in significance. Patrons and artists began to place greater emphasis on the naturalistic world around them, of which *they experienced themselves as centre*. Such an approach is fundamentally different from the unrealistic, unnatural settings to be seen in medieval/Gothic paintings. Martin Kemp points out that these, and many similar ideas, which were expressed by

Leonardo in the late 1480s are not original to him, for they take their ultimate cue from a statement in Aristotle's *On the Soul.* Leonardo's studies in science and engineering are as impressive and innovative as his artistic work. They were recorded in notebooks comprising some 13,000 pages of notes and drawings, which 'fuse' science and art. His approach to science was an observational one. He sought to understand a phenomenon by describing and depicting it in utmost detail, and did not emphasize either experiments or theoretical explanation.[222]

Masaccio's *Tribute Money*, (1425) was the first painting which portrayed continuous space. It should also be noted that in this majestic fresco the diminution of trees, together with the lightening of colours, blurring of forms and loss of details, showed the use of aerial perspective (Plate 31). Piero della Francesca uses landscape backgrounds behind his paintings of Battista Sforza and Federico da Montefeltro (c.1472) for the first time in Italian portraiture. (Plate 11.) The two landscapes depicted show typical views of the area around the city of Urbino. Piero della Francesca's *Baptism of Christ* portrays the local area around Sansepolcro. Depth and space are suggested by the river winding into the distance. Leonardo's scientific observations of nature are reflected in, for instance, the plants depicted in the background of *The Annunciation* (Plate 12). These plants, together with others, are referred to in some detail in his notebooks. Such scientific observations are also evident in *Madonna of the Rocks* (begun in 1483) where the landscape is clearly based on Leonardo's considerable knowledge of flora, geology (rocks) and water.

In a document which one or both of the brothers van Eyck illuminated during the second or third decade of the fifteenth century, the *Turin Book of Hours*, we find a true landscape painting. It shows a river bank surrounded by green, wooded hills, where a castle and smaller buildings recede in diminishing sizes into the distance. In the foreground we see Christ being baptized by John. In the middle distance a small group of ladies and gentlemen are taking their country stroll. In the background we can see a low horizon, its blue paleness revealing how distant it really is, echoing the blue reflection of the water. Here a hitherto unexpressed fidelity to nature is revealed; going hand in hand, we could say, with the coming into being of a self-conscious experience of one's individual place on the physical earth, or differently expressed, with the manifestation of the early steps towards the full development of the consciousness soul. So, the new element manifesting itself here in the first half of the fifteenth century, particularly in the work of Jan van Eyck, is that it is based on an exact observation of objects in the sense-perceptible world. The microscopic quality of Jan's vision, that is, his precise rendering of details in landscapes—also interiors, we could call to mind his painting of the betrothal of Giovanni Arnolfini and Jeanne de Chenany (1434)—is quite remarkable (Plate 13). Conrad Schöffling makes the following observations which are highly relevant in the present context:

> Like no one before him, [Jan] van Eyck was able to give his subjects, both physical objects and people, a wonderful plasticity and to instil an unprecedented significance into everyday scenes. He eschewed all forms of idealization, preferring to create *individual characters with uniquely personal physical features.*[223] [My emphasis.]

In its own way van Eyck's art was as new and revolutionary as Donatello's or Masaccio's work in Italy (see the final chapter). E.H. Gombrich in his *Story of Art* writes: 'A simple corner of the real world had suddenly been fixed on to a panel as if by magic. Here it all was—the carpet and the slippers, the rosary on the wall, the little brush beside the bed, and the fruit on the windowsill. It is as if we could pay a visit to the Arnolfini in their house.'[224] Giovanni Arnolfini, a wealthy merchant, holds Jeanne de Chenany's, his wife-to-be's right hand in his left and raises his right hand to pledge his troth to her in a ceremony before witnesses that had the full force of marriage. He looks towards the witnesses. There are two, reflected in the convex mirror on the back wall (see plate 23). The mirror itself is witness, too, to the reality of the room. It shows the top of the chest, otherwise hidden by Arnolfini's fur-trimmed coat. Everything in this depicted room is an exact transcription of reality: the bottle glass in the window, the apples on the chest, the wooden sandals for outdoor use, the grained floorboards, the gathering up of the fiancée's dress in the fashionable pregnant look then current in France where she was brought up. Jan van Eyck seems to have been keen on reproducing every minute detail in his picture to such an extent that we almost seem able to count the little dog's hairs.

In 2005 an exhibition was mounted in the Queen's Gallery, Buckingham Palace, of 51 outstanding examples of Dutch paintings of the seventeenth century, the Golden Age. Some 200 years or so after Jan van Eyck's intimate painting, we find that genre painting—the depiction of everyday life—flourished in the newly formed Dutch United Provinces. The wonder of the seventeenth century Dutch works shown in this exhibition—and of many others to be found throughout the world—and the reason for their near universal appeal down the ages, is that they show us a society *looking at itself.* It is an art which, at its greatest, seems to celebrate small things and small moments. A fine example in the Queen's collection illustrating the points just made is Jan Steen's *A Woman at her Toilet.* It shows a woman's everyday activity with unsparing candour (Plate 14).

The leaders of Renaissance taste in fifteenth century Florence were keen buyers of Flemish paintings and tapestries depicting pastoral activities. However, it was Italian artistic theory which ultimately made the idea of landscape painting well known. In Alberti's *Ten Books on Architecture,* probably written about 1450—the contents of which were known to both painters and architects in Florence before it was finally published in 1486—we find a chapter[225] on the decoration of buildings and interiors. There we read:

> Both painting and poetry vary in kind. The type that portrays the great deeds of great men, worthy of memory, differs from that which describes the habits of private citizens, and again from that depicting the life of the peasants. The first, which is majestic in character, should be used for public buildings and the dwellings of the great, while the last mentioned will be suitable for gardens, for it is the most pleasing of all. Our minds are cheered beyond measure by the sight of paintings depicting the delightful countryside, harbours, fishing, hunting, swimming, the games of shepherds—flowers and verdure . . .[226]

We see, in this passage, an emphasis on *human activity* as depicted in Flemish paintings and tapestries. Alberti is not, in short, concerned with the idea of 'pure' landscape. Moreover he does not see these paintings—and tapestries—as mere decorations but as art to be treasured for its psychological effect. This is made even more explicit in another passage of Alberti's book on architecture:

> Those who suffer from fever are offered much relief by the sight of painted fountains, rivers and running brooks, a fact which anyone can put to the test; for if by chance he lies in bed one night unable to sleep, he need only turn his imagination on limpid waters and fountains which he had seen at one time or another, or perhaps some lake, and his dry feeling will disappear all at once and sleep will come upon him as the sweetest of slumbers.

It is illuminating, especially in the context of the philosophy prevalent in the thinking prevailing in the Florentine Academy in the fifteenth century, to find that Plato stated in *The Republic* that 'all grace of movement and harmony of living—the moral disposition of the soul itself—are determined by aesthetic feeling, by the recognition of rhythm and harmony'.[227]

> ... enter largely into painting and all similar workmanship, into weaving and embroidery, into architecture, as well as the whole manufacture of utensils in general; nay, into the constitution of living bodies, and of all plants; for in all these things, gracefulness or ungracefulness [*sic*] finds place. And the absence of grace, and rhythm, and harmony, is closely allied to an evil style and an evil character; whereas their presence is allied to, and expressive of, the opposite character, which is brave and sober minded.[228]

All through the fourteenth century petitions from associations and individual citizens of towns in Tuscany had been submitted to the governing body to improve conditions in the city. Laws were passed to compel owners of high buildings to either reduce them in height or to pull them down altogether so that more light could reach the streets below. However, these laws seemed to have little effect. Nevertheless the desire for wider spaces, for harmonious and beautiful buildings set in adequate surroundings, remained a widespread ambition of the people of Tuscany. Rosa Maria Letts quotes an eloquently worded proclamation issuing from Siena in 1309 which maintained that 'those who are charged with the government of the city should pay particular attention to its beautification. An important and essential ingredient of a *civilized community* being a park or a meadow for the pleasure of both citizens and foreigners.'[229]

Alberti, who understood the wider political meaning of Brunelleschi's building, said that the dome represented a space that was 'large enough to contain all the people of Tuscany'.[230]

> People have been seized by a passion for 'interior space'. They can no longer stand to be somewhere without being 'inside'. And so it happens that interior spaces are formed even in places where one is actually 'outside': *yards* or *courts* become an important component of the architectural activity of the period. We have only to think of the narrow, compact, spaceless way in which the medieval town or castle was built to sense how everything widens out now from the inside. Suddenly everyone feels the need for space: private, bounded space in which he can breathe and whose boundaries are his own property because he has established them himself. The town, as a

single structural unit, is seized by this passion, too. As a form for the 'inner space' of its *self-awareness* [my emphasis] it creates the *market place*, with its arcades and colonnades, which is no more than a widened out courtyard.[231]

12. Portraits

> Ever since the Renaissance, the western world has operated on the belief that human beings are highly individual and that the exciting thing about being a human being is matching your individuality with who other people are.... In 1300 nobody painted self-portraits; yet the self-portrait has been a very important kind of work of art since the Renaissance because of the artist's sense that he wants to look inside himself and outside at the same time.
>
> *(Jacob Bronowski)*[232]

The first painted portraits were the Greco-Roman panels carried out in encaustic from the first to third century AD. The Fayum mummy portraits come under this heading.[233] The surviving paintings are predominantly from the Fayum region in Roman Egypt; they are interesting not only for historical reasons but also for their vivid humanity:

> And the secret of this is to be found in the way the artists had concentrated on the main features—eyes, mouth and general shape of the head. The eyes especially in each case magnetically hold the attention. There is no attempt at natural lighting or at the illusion of reality at which some modern painters aim, but the absence of these qualities seems to add a special force and lifelike character to the essentials so firmly grasped.[234] [Plate 15.]

In the present context it is relevant to note a fundamental difference between sculptured portraits typical of the Greek classical period and those emerging during the early Italian Renaissance. Whereas portraits of the early Renaissance may be said to reflect the physical human being known to his or her contemporaries, this could not be claimed for those of the Greek classical period. Even when individual human beings were portrayed they seemed to have an aura of divinity. The sculptors who portrayed Homer neither knew nor cared what he looked like: they were portraying poetry, inspiration, wisdom. Philosophers are occasionally marked by strong individuality, but on the whole they tend to merge into a composite portrayal of wisdom and learning. Of the Hellenistic age, however, we may perceive a foreshadowing of the portraiture of the Renaissance.[235]

In the Middle Ages, when attention was focussed on religious subjects, there was very little attempt at individual portraiture, but from the fourteenth century onwards the practice grew of including in the group compositions of altarpieces portraits of the donor and benefactor of the Church.[236] During the Middle Ages the donor figures were portrayed on a much smaller scale than the sacred figures. Often, even surprisingly late into the Renaissance, the donor portraits, especially when a whole family is shown, will be at a much smaller scale than the principal figures, in defiance of linear perspective. However, from the early years of the fifteenth century, this is the exception rather than the rule.

Before the fifteenth century a physical likeness may not have often been attempted, or achieved; the individuals depicted may in any case often not been available to the artist, or even alive. By the mid fifteenth century this was no longer the case, and donors, and other notable men and women of whom other likenesses survive, can often be seen to be carefully portrayed. Nevertheless, even then, as Rab Hatfield maintains, the artist of the quattrocento did not always feel bound to present his subject's physical likeness.

> It often happens that the artist has taken the actual appearance of his subject into account but also made adjustments in his image in order to convey qualities such as the subject's personality, character, status, emotions and so on. The range of these adjustments may in some instances be so great that different portraits of the same man seem to represent entirely different persons.[237]

In one of his letters Ficino wrote:

> I have often looked for myself . . . I have gazed at this face in the mirror . . . but I could never say I have . . . seen myself. For when I seek myself, it is exactly the same Marsilio that is both seeker and sought . . . it is spirit alone I seek, since I seek myself, who am indeed pure spirit . . .[238]

Pamela Tudor-Craig observes that there lies the essential difference between Italian and northern European portraiture in the fifteenth century. For instance, the Flemish portrait of this period was admired for its detailed veracity. Its Italian counterpart, though equally detailed also attempted to suggest, in addition to the outer appearance of the sitter, his or her interior feelings and emotions, 'those less tangible qualities of character, and even, maybe, in works of genius, a spiritual dimension'.[239] Fundamentally, however, the function of portraiture was to capture the appearance of a particular person at the time of depiction, thereby creating a permanent image that would endure long beyond the subject's lifetime. Portraiture developed during a period of cultural and intellectual change that shook the foundations of collective medieval communities and engendered a new positive view of the individual.

It is clear from our considerations hitherto that, increasingly as the fifteenth century progressed, art, particularly paintings, reflected man's world: buildings were planned in accordance with the proportions of the ideal human body as propounded by Vitruvius; literature celebrated man's achievements and various qualities; the growing awareness of nature, of the world around him; preoccupation with human activities; the building up of an ideal toward which man should aspire to realize by bettering his mind, all this inevitably led to an increased sense of *individualism*, of a deeper and clearer *consciousness of self*, and a firm experience of 'dignity'. The last three assertions regarding man find a wonderful confirmation in Masaccio's rendering of the Holy Trinity on the left wall of Santa Maria Novella Church in Florence in 1427. This fresco is more than six metres high and three metres wide. It represents God the Father holding Christ on the Cross. Between the two a dove hovers silently, representing the Holy Spirit. The Madonna and St John are at the feet of Christ. This sacred group is situated in an architectural structure, a chapel, which ideally separates them from us, onlookers, as well as from the two people kneeling at the bottom of the scene. The married couple Cardoni, the actual purchasers of the fresco, are also present in the painting. He is dressed in red, she in blue. They are depicted not only in prayer, but also, in accord with the consciousness of the dignity of man, and in contrast to medieval portrayals, of the same size as Mary, the Mother of Jesus Christ, and St John. Moreover, they serve as a reminder to posterity of the glory of the generosity of their family. (Plate 16.)

A mere eight or nine years later we find this stress on the *'worth' and dignity of man* even more clearly expressed when we turn to Jan van Eyck's painting of *The Virgin of Chancellor Rolin* (c.1435). Nicolas Rolin, Chancellor of Burgundy and Brabant, commissioned this work. He was a man of humble background. He was highly intelligent and eventually rose to hold the highest office of state. Jan van Eyck painted him when he was already in his 60s. The chancellor's face is marked by the heavy responsibilities he has borne for over 40 years, and fascinates the viewer with the sense of energy and will-power which it projects.(Plate 17.) Rolin kneels in prayer on the left of the composition just a few feet distant from the seated figure of the Virgin. He is portrayed as being more or less of the same size as the Mother of the Jesus child and in the same physical space, not, as was the case in Masaccio's *Holy Trinity*, 'outside' it. In short, the chancellor is fully conscious of the dignity of his humanhood.

Here, in the light of the specific theme we are concerned with in these pages, it is relevant to note that it was in 1420 that the brothers van Eyck settled in Ghent. Hubert, the elder of the two, died in 1426, Jan 14 years later. In the short period of 20 years the human mind, represented by these two men in northern Europe, had found, in painting, the most ideal expression of its thoughts and beliefs, the most physiognomic expression of faces, not the noblest, maybe, but the first correct manifestation of human bodies in their exact forms, the first realistic picture of the sky, of the surrounding landscape, of clothes, and so on. Eugene Fromentin elaborating upon the work of the van Eyck brothers and referring to the human mind during the short period in question states: 'It had created a living art.'[240]

Realistic portraiture, what Kenneth Clark curiously spoke of as being 'the use of the accidents of each individual face to reveal inner life,'[241] was not a Florentine 'invention'. It first made its appearance in Flanders in the work of Jan van Eyck. 'No one', Clark continues, 'has looked at the human face with a more dispassionate eye and recorded his findings with a more delicate hand.' Interestingly, Clark reminds us, many of those whose portraits were painted by Jan van Eyck were Italians. That of Giovanni di Nicolao Arnolfini and his wife, Giovanna Cenami (Jeanne de Chenany), both from Lucca, painted in 1434, is a wonderful and telling example of van Eyck's remarkable sensitivity. His exploration of an individual personality extended beyond the face. In his double portrait of Arnolfini and his wife he meticulously, lovingly, records numerous details of their daily personal life; their wooden pattens, their little dog of nameless breed, their convex mirror and magnificent brass chandelier.[242] (Plate 13.)

In one of Masaccio's frescoes in the Brancacci Chapel *The Resurrection of the Son of Theophilos and Saint Peter on a Throne*[243] he introduced contemporary figures unrelated to the biblical event including a group in which he portrayed himself and fellow artists; from right to left, Brunelleschi in a black hood, Masolino da Panicale, Masaccio himself, and Leon Battista Alberti. (Plate 18.)

A fine example of an Italian double portrait can be seen in the Louvre.

It was painted towards the end of the fifteenth century by the Florentine, Domenico Ghirlandaio, and is known as *An Old Man and his Grandson.*[244] The artist has not only portrayed the two figures with great tenderness, but also conveyed the deep affection between them. The boy is gently snuggling up to the old man. He is looking upwards, seeking the old man's eyes. He clearly cannot avoid but see and, judging by the boy's expression of astonishment, the enormous nose projecting towards him. There is a certain warmth which radiates between the old man and the boy. The boy's left hands rests gently on the old man's right side. The bright red pigment Ghirlandaio used for the garments and cap, conjures forth a richness that contrasts with the grey wall behind. The two figures seem to merge into one. (Plate 19.)

This picture is a wonderful expression of a unity born of love.

Another portrait by Ghirlandaio dating from 1490 is that of Giovanna Tornabuoni.[245] She is idealized to the extent of becoming an 'icon' of beauty for young Florentine girls. The delightful young woman stands out, in a clear contrast of light against dark, from the black niche in the background. Her reserved beauty is fittingly expressed in the formal clarity of the composition.[246] (Plate 20.)

In one of his great frescoes in the Dominican church Santa Maria Novella, *Angel Appearing to Zacharias*, executed in the late 1480s, Ghirlandaio grouped many important personalities of his age around the two biblical protagonists. On the left, from the viewers' point of view, there is a series of contemporary Neoplatonists. Their heads all at the same level continues the row of classical heads in the relief behind them—this is Ghirlandaio's way of presenting Neoplatonism as a continuation of the classical intellectual tradition. On the right, the intellectuals of Florence are standing together. Giorgio Vasari (1511–74), architect, painter and art historian[247] identified them as the Platonist Marsilio Ficino, the poet and orator Cristoforo Landino and the humanist Agnolo Poliziano. The profile head is either that of the contemporary Greek Platonist Demetrio Greco or Gentile de'Becchi.[248] (Plate 21.) It is apposite here to quote a passage from Giovanni Corsi's *Life of Marsilio Ficino*, published in 1506, in which he gives us a glimpse of Ficino's character and appearance.

> In stature he was a little hesitant of speech and stuttered, but only in pronouncing the letter 's'; yet in his speech and appearance he was not without grace. His legs and arms, and particularly his hands, were rather long. His face was drawn forward and presented a mild and pleasing aspect; his complexion was ruddy. His hair was golden and curly and

> stood up above his forehead. . . . His health was not at all settled, for he suffered very much from a weakness of the stomach, and although he always appeared cheerful and festive in company, yet it was thought that he sat long in solitude and became as if numb with melancholy.[249]

It was particularly in their sculptured portrait busts that the Florentines could vie with the realism of such an artist as Jan van Eyck. For instance, Antonio Rossellino's[250] bust, made from a life cast,[251] of Giovanni Chellini, who died in 1462, is that of a man whose lined face reveals maturity, wisdom, gained through long experience of the pain and sorrow—also the joys—of life. He was, in fact, a medical doctor. One of his many patients was Donatello, whose life he saved. Chellini's features are rendered in great detail. Rossellino here shows an extraordinary concern with the surface texture of the face. For instance, the veins on the temple, the furrows on the forehead, the wrinkles at the corner of the eyes, all are portrayed with remarkable exactitude. However, this is far more than a mere record of a man's features. Rossellino penetrates his character with insight and sensitivity. He revealed his humour, his good nature, his knowledge of human beings and his slightly cynical view of them. (Plate 22.)

Unlike the male portraits, the female portrait busts are relatively little influenced by antiquity. Though the making of female portrait busts represented a return to antique practice, there is nothing about the female busts themselves that is specifically classical. The prime document for this is the beautiful bust of the *Lady with the Primrose* by the Florentine sculptor and painter Andrea del Verrocchio (1435–88).[252]

The self-portrait as a signature

We first witness the self-portrait as a signature in ancient Egypt. It is difficult to be absolutely certain whether some of the sculptures recovered from that period were definitely self-portraits, but because we know that portraiture was the prerogative of the rich and powerful, it is generally assumed that works containing less decorated individuals were portraits of the artists themselves. The self-portrait as a signature reappeared during the late Middle Ages and the Renaissance period. Architects of the great cathedrals would sometimes have images of themselves carved in less noticeable parts of their edifices. Two well known examples are the cathedrals at Santiago di Compostela and Prague. During the Renaissance period Lorenzo Ghiberti chiselled a self-portrait, as early as 1401, into the frame surrounding the set of bronze doors created for the Florence Baptistry. As we have indicated already, Jan van Eyck in his most influential painting of the period, *The Betrothal of the Arnolfini* (Plates 13 and 23) employed a quite unique use of the self-portrait. The young couple stand facing the viewer while exchanging their wedding vows. A mirror behind the couple, near the centre of the painting, reveals Jan van Eyck's presence, as a witness, in the room. An inscription above the mirror reads *Johannes de Eyck fuit hic* ('Jan van Eyck was here').

Rogier van der Weyden, another great Flemish painter (c.1400–64) is said to have been his own model, portraying St Luke in *St Luke Painting the Virgin*. He is also given credit for being one of the earliest portrait artists to 'tell us more about the inner life of his sitters, less about their outward appearance'. (Plate 24.) In Masaccio's fresco, *The Tribute Money*, the apostle St Thomas, to the far right of the central group, is a self-portrait as a signature of the artist. (See Plate 31.) One of the earliest artists to make self-portraiture a major part of his work was Albrecht Dürer, born in 1471. The greatest printmaker of his time, Dürer seemed intrigued by his own image and like Rembrandt, born 200 years later, sought to know himself better by studying his facial expressions. His first self-portrait dates back to his adolescence in 1484. He continued to explore himself in this way until 1522.

A stream of portraits in painting, sculpture and literature followed one another in Italy. Sometimes idealized, sometimes truthful to the point of crudity. Portrait busts and medals, pictures or written descriptions perpetuated the Renaissance man. The 'new' individual, still 'young', sometimes gauche, was searching to establish a special place in history, to fulfil a role distinguished enough to be remembered and respected by posterity.[253]

The same humanist desire for the immortality of the individual that had inspired the portrait not only produced biographies and autobiographies, but also encouraged the creation of humanist tombs. The first such tomb was produced by Bernardo in 1444. Prominent among biographers was the Florentine humanist and librarian Vespasiano da Bisticci (1421–98). His intimate acquaintance with and observation of leading figures of the quattrocento, known as the *Vite di Uomini Illustri del secolo XV* (*Lives of Illustrious Men of the Fifteenth Century*), is vividly recorded in more than 300 short biographies, celebratory of some and vitriolic towards others.[254]

13. Giotto—Masaccio—Donatello

The sculptor must represent the activities of the soul.
(Socrates to the sculptor Cliton)[255]

. . . in this [Renaissance] context Donatello may be said to have set the standard for the rest, since in himself he possessed all the qualities shared among the others. He imparted movement to his figures, giving them such vivacity and animation that they are worthy to rank both . . . with the work of the ancient world and also with that of the modern.
(Vasari, Preface to Part Two of the Lives of the Artists, *1568)*

Giotto's art broke not only with the *maniera greca* but with all previous Christian painting. Giotto di Bondone (1267–1337) fused a new visual experience of his world into the deeply symbolic and inward Byzantine tradition. His mature work shares with us the life of men and women—and of Jesus Christ—as seen and experienced in a new way. Voluminous figures move against simple landscape in colours at once soft and bright. The surprising thing is not that Byzantine art was swept away so suddenly, but that the change came so late; that, for instance, up to his time prayers were still being addressed to icons. Giotto brought to painting a power that was new in Christian art: that of locating, without sacrilege, a sacred scene in a world resembling the world of human beings.[256] Untrammelled by any conventional arrangement of the elements of appearance, he handled them freely so as to express, through them, the Christian message latent in all the created world.[257] It was Giotto who brought into painting attempts to render nature, representations of the Italian countryside, realistically. Although imperfectly achieved, they were nevertheless truer than those of the Byzantines. Another quality of his that the cognoscenti of the Renaissance much admired was the 'lifelikeness' of his figures. He introduced into painting the practice of drawing human beings as they look in a solid body. Giotto was the first artist to paint human beings in such a way that they possessed weight.

So, painting in the thirteenth century had been largely dominated by Byzantine influence. The olive skinned, slant-eyed, icon-like Madonnas of the Florentine artist Cimabue and the Sienese painter Duccio di Buoninsegna (1260–1319) are refined expressions of established tradition. In comparison Giotto towers like a giant, even if by fifteenth century standards he was naïve and primitive. His figures have, to use Bernard Berenson's expressive phrase, 'tactile values',[258] you feel that you could touch them, walk round them, that they could walk round you. You could meet them on equal terms, as it were. Giotto used with great economy light, shade, colour, and strongly featured men and women to impart this sense of solid form and three-dimensional space. In time depth would be provided with mathematical precision, but Giotto was able to do without the mathematics (geometry) involved. As just indicated, Giotto painted realistic figures, who stood in stark contrast to the 'flat' figures found in Italian paintings hitherto.[259] The telling comparison to evidence this point is to compare Giotto's *Maestà* (c.1310) painted for the church of Ognissanti, Florence (Plate 25); with Cimabue's *Maestà* (c.1280) originally on the high altar of the church of Santa Trinita in Florence (Plate 26); and the *Maestà* of the Sienese Duccio (1285) from the Rucellai chapel in the Church of Santa Maria Novella, Florence (Plate 27); all three of which are in Room 2 of the Uffizi Gallery. Of the three it is only the Mother of the Jesus child depicted in Giotto's painting who looks at us, communicates with humankind; those shown by Cimabue and Duccio gaze out into a non-spatial realm.

As mentioned already, Cimabue was strongly influenced by the Byzantine tradition. Both the Virgin and Child are portrayed as medieval figures. Neither fully represents a living and breathing human being. In particular the mother of the Jesus child does not gaze into the earthly world; does not seek contact with those around and in front of her. We may even wonder whether she really physically occupies the throne. The angels on either side of the throne upon which she is placed are rendered stiffly, balanced in their placement, but still resulting in a work that conforms to the non-naturalistic, two-dimensional tradition of Byzantine art. We need to remember here that Orthodox icons are not intended to be looked at as naturalistic works of art. The painters of Orthodox icons, which, as just indicated, were the models for such pre-Renaissance artists as Cimabue, are not 'illustrators in the sense that we today in the west [since the Renaissance] speak of illustrations in religious paintings', we learn from John Baggley, who also makes it clear that although 'not all icon painters have the same depth of spiritual experience and understanding, just as they may not all have the same artistic ability or competence; . . . however brilliant or pedestrian they and their work may be, the intention is the same: to externalize the sacred tradition and to enable the beholder to enter into the unseen world of the Spirit which transcends and yet penetrates the world of matter, of flesh'.[260] In the *Maestà* of Duccio the pattern is similar and the appearance of both Mother and Child, too, but treated with a poetic delicacy which is invariably found in the school of Siena. One notable difference is that the portrayal of the child is softer and freer.

The emergence of Giotto may be said to signal the changes we witness a century later—the early Renaissance in Florence. His style of painting broke radically from the past. Sometimes called the 'father of western pictorial art', his painting turned from the flatter, more iconic Byzantine style to a more naturalistic approach. A firm proponent of using observation of nature, his painting emphasized some major characteristics of modern representational art. In his *Maestà* (Uffizi) (Plate 25) there is a definite conciliation of a mystical vision with a more human dimension. This is shown in the more realistic depiction of the throne in space, the solid corporeality of all the figures, the controlled but intense emotional relationships, beautifully expressed by means of the gestures of the hands, the intensity of the gaze of wonder and love of angels and saints on either side of the throne. The Mother is a being of flesh and blood; she is not looking into a 'spaceless' region, but seeks the eyes and hearts of all men and women in the world around her. We may experience something like this as we stand and meditate before this mighty *Maestà*: through the warmth which rays out from her, she also seeks to draw humankind before the blessing of the Divine Being who, in 30 years time, at the Baptism in the Jordan, will incarnate in the body of Jesus. Giotto's *Lamentation*—one of his frescoes in the Arena Chapel (Padua)—reveals an emotional eloquence not found in the art of earlier times. (Plate 28.) It is a scene of grief, yet there are different, individual reactions to the death of Christ. Mary, clinging to the body of her son with one arm draped across his chest, searches his countenance as if to penetrate the veil that prevails between life and death; John, the Beloved Disciple, flings his arms out in protesting disbelief; Mary Magdalene gazes in inward, tender sorrow at the beloved feet she had once washed with her tears; each of the others react in similarly individual ways; and above, the angels give vent to their sorrow.

It is fascinating to read the work by the humanist and historian, Matteo Palmieri (1406–1475) for which he is best known, *Della Vita Civile* (*On Civic Life*), composed in 1429 and circulated between 1435–1440. The following is a passage from this work which is particularly relevant to our theme.[261]

> For some centuries now the noble arts, which were well understood and practised by our ancient forebears, have been so deficient that it is shameful how little they have produced and with what little honour.... Before Giotto, painting was dead and figure painting laughable. Having been restored by him, sustained by his disciples and passed on to others, painting has now become a most worthy art practised by many.

Palmieri then makes various statements regarding sculpture, architecture and literature and goes on to state, in somewhat flowery language:

> ... today we see our Leonardo Bruni, [c.1369–1444, leading humanist and a chancellor of Florence] ... sent into the world as the father and ornament of letters, the resplendent light of Latin elegance, to restore the sweetness of the Latin language to mankind. For this reason anyone of intelligence should thank God for being born in these times, in which we enjoy a more splendid flowering of the arts than at any other time in the last thousand years.

For 100 years there was little or no advance on Giotto's innovating skill, only imitation. Then, all at once, as Italian art seemed to be drifting into its own version of the Gothic, the promise of Giotto was fulfilled in one of the greatest of all Florentine painters—Masaccio (1401–1428). His frescoes in the Brancacci Chapel of the Florentine church of Santa Maria del Carmine were probably painted between 1425 and 1427. Right from the earliest years of their completion, these frescoes became 'the axis on which Florentine painting rotated'[262] and were revered by generations of artists—including such giants of the High Renaissance as Michelangelo, Leonardo da Vinci and Raphael. His remarkable abilities were not, however, like Giotto's exercised in isolation. From 1400 onwards there were two other artists of outstanding ability closely associated with him: the sculptor Donatello and the architect Brunelleschi. In fact, Masaccio's art developed under the influence of the new ideas, represented in Florence, by the architect Brunelleschi and the sculptor Donatello. Brunelleschi had devoted lengthy studies to perspective, which had previously been applied very imperfectly. At the same time Donatello was showing by his sculptures that 'the study of antiquity could . . . be combined with a vigorous, almost popular, realism'.[263] Giorgio Vasari (1511–1574) has a phrase about Masaccio which may sound trivial on first hearing. He wrote in *Lives of the Artists*: 'Masaccio perceived that the best painters follow nature as closely as possible'. One may ask why the same could not have been said of Giotto. There is, however, as Wölfflin reminds us, a deeper meaning in this simple sentence. What appears to us so obvious and natural now—that representational painting should give the viewer the impression of physical reality—was not always so. The whole Middle Ages made no attempt to 'follow nature'. Giotto took the preliminary steps towards such an attempt, but it was Masaccio who broke through to 'the imitation of things as they are'. In Florence, one should see Giotto and Masaccio immediately after one other, so as to appreciate the difference in all its clarity. To begin with, we realize that Masaccio has complete mastery of spatial problems. For the first time in the history of painting the picture becomes a stage, constructed by establishing a unified point of vision; a space in which people, trees, houses, have their specific place, which can be geometrically calculated. In Giotto everything is still 'glued together', to use Heinrich Wölfflin's vivid expression.[264] He, Giotto, superimposes head upon head without allowing himself sufficient room for all the bodies, and the architecture of the background is without any real relation in scale to the human figures. Masaccio shows possible, habitable houses, realistically related in terms of space. Step by step, as it were, we are drawn into the depth of space, where everything is clearly set out 'in layers' one behind the other. This 'new' art may also be seen very clearly in, for instance, the Church of Santa Maria Novella in Florence in the fresco *The Trinity* (c.1425–1427) where four zones are developed in depth, with the strongest spatial effect being achieved by the use of architecture and overlapping planes. Masaccio is said to have consulted with Brunelleschi prior to undertaking the creation of this painting.[265] 'The way in which the figures and the architecture are put in a coherent spatial relationship is remarkable. (See Plate 16.) The coffered vault—clearly influenced by Brunelleschi's Barbadori—Chapel of the Church of Santa Felicità—gives an amazing impression of depth.

From what has been said hitherto, it is clear this fresco has in itself all the characteristics of new art: a perfect perspective element; an architectural frame in which every single element—column, capital, arch, vault—derives from models of ancient Roman architecture. Finally, there is a clear realism in the representation of the bodies; here we may notice, for instance, the small detail that the male Cardoni is painted with his ear bent due to his red hood pressing down on it and the expressions of the characters—no longer icon-like, lifeless, as in traditional medieval style. Masaccio also shows a grasp of human personality and his ability to portray the reaction of the individual to the impact of great spiritual events with a gravity and a grandeur, rivalled only in the work of Donatello. Underneath the married couple there is an altar on which a skeleton lies and on which, facing us, is a horizontal inscription which quite clearly states in Italian: *Io fui già quell che voi siete e quell che son voi ancor sarete*, which, in English reads: 'I was what you are, and what I am you shall be'. We may say here that the skeleton serves three symbolic functions: as Death himself, as a reminder of the transience of life, and as Adam, who embodies the promise of salvation since he was the first man to be redeemed by Christ's blood. Masaccio turned the Christ of the fourteenth century, a suffering symbolic Christ, into a real human being. He does this both in the *Trinity*, and in *The Tribute Money* in the Brancacci Chapel, where Christ, surrounded by and one with humankind, with us, is portrayed here as the central point of the natural world. Christ's head embraces the vanishing point of Masaccio's perspective system. Christ and we, so to speak, are, together, the centre of reality. This is, of course, in keeping with the whole movement and impulse of Christian Humanism that was developing so strongly in Florence in the years of Masaccio's working life. We, as spectators standing in front of Masaccio's great fresco, *The Holy Trinity*, in Santa Maria Church are called upon to enter into the 'space' we see before us. The Madonna is indeed turned towards us directing our attention to her Son on the Cross. With this fresco we can experience a work of art which, unlike those of the young artist's predecessors, is interactive with us. We could experience the 'glimmerings' of such interaction when, as mentioned already, we stand before Giotto's *Majestà* in the Uffizi.

According to traditional iconography in painting classical building forms, such as we see here,—the fluted pilasters and the Corinthian capitals, the architrave, the pillars with the Ionic capitals and the panelled barrel vault—are not part of either the motif of the Throne of Grace or the Crucifixion. With the former, Florentines of the early fifteenth century would expect to see a gold background as an indication of its sacred nature, instead they, and we today, see here 'the greatest conscientiousness in the reproduction of natural forms, clarity of geometrical structure and the insignia of the classical architectural alphabet'.[266] The surprise of the people of the fifteenth century must have been great when the fresco was unveiled, simulating a hole in the wall through which they looked into a new chapel in Brunelleschi's building style. They would also have been astonished to see that the donors, human citizens of Florence, are depicted as being of the same physical size as the Holy Mother and St John, in contrast to the medieval tradition. Men and women of fifteenth century Florence are conscious of themselves as fully incarnated 'earth beings' who not only manifest respect for 'higher beings', but also for themselves and each other. Beside this work Giotto's paintings do look flat. Giotto used only quite weak shadow on his forms and, as Wölfflin comments, 'not because he did not see them, but because it seemed to him superfluous to go into the matter deeply. He regarded them as a disturbing accident in the picture, which could add nothing to the significance of the matter.' For Masaccio, on the other hand, it is clear that light and shadow were elements of primary significance for, to quote again from Wölfflin, 'the way he sought to render the essence, the corporeality, in the full strength of natural effect the decisive thing here is the way in which he gives an entirely new impression in dealing merely with the detail of a head, marking the limits of the form by a few massive strokes, so that the volume is rendered with unheard of force.'[267] Furthermore, and this is of particular importance, for it confirms the contention that art in Florence at the beginning of the fifteenth century gives manifest expression to the emergence of the consciousness soul; for the first time in the history of painting human beings are portrayed *standing firmly on the physical earth.* Here we may compare his portrayal of the *Expulsion from Paradise* (Plate 29) with Masolino da Panicale's fresco of *The Temptation of Adam and Eve* (Plate 30), painted 1424–25, on the wall in the Brancacci Chapel opposite that of Masaccio's fresco. Masolino's two figures do not have the same firm relationship to the earth beneath their feet;[268] nor, incidentally, do they show anything like the same emotional intensity. Masolino paints a gentle world in the non-sculptural style of medieval illuminations and altarpieces. His nudes are placid, as befits Adam and Eve in Paradise. Even the human face on the serpent has the sweetness that characterizes Masolino's work.

Masaccio and Masolino da Panicale (1383–1447), who were near-contemporaries and collaborators in the same scheme of mural decoration, might be thought to be two or three generations apart. Masolino's *Temptation of Adam and Eve* in the Brancacci chapel exhales the charm of the lovely nudes of Italy before it attained its historical maturity. The most striking difference in the approach of the two artists may be seen in the courtly elegance of Masolino's Adam and Eve in contrast to Masaccio's huddled, weeping figures. Masolino's soft, pearly flesh serves as a foil to the vigorously modelled, sculptural anatomy of Masaccio's Adam and Eve. The latter not only show the solidity and firmness of the physical body, but also the truly human expressions of guilt and suffering.[269] Masaccio reveals in his work a remarkably sharpened feeling for personality, and an emphasis on the individual. Giotto, it is true, differentiated his figures yet they are only general distinctions; in Masaccio's *The Tribute Money*, we find clearly marked individual characters. How different Peter's stature and facial expression are from those from the Beloved Disciple, John! For the first time, at the dawn of the fifteenth century, the interest is now not only in the 'character's' head, but in the full range of individual pose and movement. It was this fresco by Masaccio which inspired Alberti to pronounce in his treatise *On Painting* that 'a "historia", then, will move the souls of those who look at it when the men painted there display the motion of their own souls to the highest degree'. *The Tribute Money* is a multiple narrative. Christ and the Apostles have arrived at Capernaum. This is a Roman city and they are asked to pay an entrance toll of tribute. As Jews, in their own homeland, they argue—in the central episode—about the rights and wrongs of this imperialist imposition with the gatekeeper, whose back and arms eloquently declare his surprise at their obstinacy. Christ cuts the argument short. He tells the indignant Peter to cast a line in the lake of Galilee—as he does in the episode on the left, crouching to haul it out—'and when thou hast opened its mouth, thou shalt find a piece of money: that take, and give unto them for me and thee' (Matthew 17:24–27). In the third episode Peter dumps the coin in the gatekeeper's hand. The story is enacted on the outskirts of a credible town, where buildings soar up beyond the border of the fresco. We look past buildings and figures into a landscape of lake, trees, hills, and cloudy sky which do not just hint at physical reality but show it. The landscape recedes evenly, changing in tone and clarity. Each individual figure in Masaccio's masterpiece has his own space. The young artist has depicted the real physical world as our eyes perceive it. (Plate 31.) We could compare Masaccio's great fresco with, say, Duccio's *Way to Calvary* in the Museo dell'Opera del Duomo in Siena (Plate 32), which clearly does not show such a realistic portraying of space; one wonders, in fact, how the individuals in the crowd following and surrounding Christ can spatially exist in relation to one another.

Moving again to the Netherlands and moving from the outer, open countryside shown in Masaccio's fresco depicting the Tribute Money to an indoor single room—Jan van Eyck (c.1370–1441) in his *The Betrothal of the Arnolfini* of 1434—just about seven years after Masaccio's great fresco—bears witness to the real world in remarkable detail; in contrast to Masaccio's concentration on the whole rather than the minute details. Masaccio's and van Eyck's paintings are wonderful documents of a new age of realistic perception, which differed more in approach then intention. The southern artists of Jan van Eyck's generation, the Florentine masters of Brunelleschi's circle, had developed a method by which nature could be represented in a picture with almost scientific accuracy. They began with a framework of perspective lines, and they built up the human body through their knowledge of anatomy and of the laws of foreshortening. Jan van Eyck took the opposite way. He achieved the illusion of nature by patiently adding detail upon detail till his whole picture became like a mirror of the visible world. Gombrich states:

> This difference between northern and Florentine art remained important for many years. It is a fair guess to say that any work which excels in the representation of the beautiful surface of things, of flowers, jewels or fabric, will be by a northern artist, most probably by an artist of the Netherlands; while a painting with bold outlines, clear perspective and a sure mastery of the beautiful human body, will be Italian.[270]

Sculpture

However, it was not a painter but a Florentine sculptor who was the first full exponent of the new spirit.[271] Masaccio's early death at the age of 27 cut short what he had to say, but Donatello's[272] long career—he was born about 1386 and died 1466—spread over the whole first half of the fifteenth century. Although Brunelleschi was the originator of the 'new style', Donatello was the great driving force behind its development. And it was from the ideas he put into practice that the whole picture of Florentine quattrocento sculpture unfolded. Already in his early period in Florence, that is, until 1443, Donatello laid great stress on increasing the realism and impact of the work of art by reducing the psychological barrier between the work and its beholder. Much of the universal and enduring value of Donatello's art lies in the manner in which he interpreted and portrayed character. This he achieved by endowing his figures with increasingly strong personalities, as can be seen when the marble statue of *David* (Plate 33) begun in 1408, is compared with the *Zuccone* (see Plate 9) completed in 1433–36.

The soft, flowing drapery of this early *David* forms a clear contrast to the almost brutal expressiveness of *Zuccone's* robes.[273] The same characteristics appear in Donatello's early reliefs, with the addition of the scientific perspective he developed in association with Brunelleschi and Masaccio. The relief of *St George and the Dragon* (Plate 34), dating from shortly before 1420, is the earliest example of perspective which had been planned scientifically. The effect is enhanced by the use of the *stiacciato* relief, a pictorial technique of strong modelling in very low relief which Donatello developed to give a still greater illusion of depth.[274]

Donatello's naturalistically polychromed, wooden figure of the freely standing *Penitent Magdalene* (late 1430s-mid 1440s) is represented praying; her spiritual concentration is imbued with profound vitality, energy. She is clothed only in her own hair; her usual attributes—skull, cross, and even the familiar ointment jar—have been omitted by the sculptor so that her character and emotional state may be emphasized. This figure is one of Donatello's most powerful works; her concentration on an other-worldly goal is so powerful that the observer is drawn into her experience.[275] (Plate 35.) The New Testament tells us of Mary Magdalene's part in the Passion, and Jacobus de Voragine's *Legenda Aurea* (*Golden Legend*)[276] of her life after the Resurrection, when, according to Voragine, she retreated into the wilds of southern France, for 30 years living a life of fasting and penance as a mountain hermit. She discarded her sumptuous garments and eventually was clothed only in her own long hair. Donatello's representation accords well with the saint's legend, as well as with the text from Proverbs (31:30) read during the Office of St Mary Magdalene; 'Favour is deceitful and beauty is vain; but a woman that feareth the Lord, she shall be praised'. Bennett and Wilkins observe: 'A memory of her worldliness survives in her pose, which must be ranked among the most beautiful and subtle instances of *contrapposto* in the history of sculpture.'[277]

Donatello's bronze *David* (Plate 36) shows us clear similarities to classical sculpture; this is particularly communicated in the balanced distribution of weight in the figure, and its nudity.[278] The sculptor also shows us a victorious hero who is but a slight youth standing relaxed and *self-absorbed*. His sensuously treated nudity is set off by elaborate boots and floppy hat. As Bennett and Wilkins point out, 'it is no wonder the *David* is also among Donatello's most controversial works. But one thing is certain, this is a revolutionary statue in the history of sculpture. To the best of present knowledge, he is the first life-sized free-standing nude figure in over a millennium.'[279] As a free-standing life-size nude Donatello's bronze *David* is undoubtedly one of the most important sculptures of the

Italian early Renaissance. No matter from which side one approaches the work, one always sees a figure of extremely harmonious grace and always playful lightness. As Vasari remarked, Donatello seems to have based the figure less on the repertoire of forms in sculptural models, than on a visualization of a living body: 'This figure is so natural in its vivacity and softness that artists find it hardly possible to believe it was not moulded on the living form.'

The young David, future king of Israel, is one of the most important heroes of the Old Testament. Donatello represents him after the completion of his heroic act. Donatello's *David* conforms neither to a generalized Renaissance ideal, nor to a specific antique type. It may seem very strange that Donatello should represent the great hero to be not only no more than a youth but also of an essentially non-heroic, or even anti-heroic, nature.[280] However, Donatello's interpretation is in keeping with the biblical text, which clearly refers to the beauty and youthfulness of Jesse's youngest son:

> And Samuel said unto Jesse, 'Are here all your children?' And he said, 'There remaineth yet the youngest, and, behold, he keepeth the sheep . . .' And he sent and brought him in. Now he was ruddy, and withal of a beautiful countenance, and goodly to look to. (I Samuel 16:11–12.)

David's nudity facing Goliath is in accord with I Samuel 17: 38–39 which tells us how he had first put on the armour of Saul and then later taken it off, having decided not to wear armour. Also David's non-heroic behaviour is clarified, since he declared, before the battle, that the victory would not be his:

> I come to thee in the name of the Lord of hosts. . . . This day will the Lord deliver thee into mine hand; and I will smite thee, and take thine head from thee; . . . And all this assembly shall know that the Lord saveth not with a sword and spear: for the battle is the Lord's, and He will give you into our hands (I Samuel 17: 45–47).

'Donatello's *David*, then, is not only consistent with the traditional texts, but appropriately emphasizes God's role in the boy's unexpected victory.'[281] The hat *David* is wearing is most likely made of straw. Shepherds working in the fields in warm weather wore such hats. The boots David wears appear to be military gear. However, it seems plausible that they may rather be strong shepherd's boots, since he had rejected armour. Emil Bock observes that:

> Regardless of whether individual traits in the story of David's battle with the giant Goliath are intended to refer to physically real events or not, we have in them a picture of the collision of two soul-natures. One belongs to the past, the other is just appearing on the stage of history. Perhaps the main point in the sequence of outer occurrences was the magic spell of fear with which the Philistines tried to overcome the Israelites was broken by David's clear power of thought, and that owing to David's cleverness the enemy's army was brought to the point of destroying itself—something that would be expressed in the picture of Goliath being beheaded with his own sword.[282]

The youthful David was a subject dear to the hearts of the Florentine Renaissance—above all for Donatello and Michelangelo. In David they saw the embodiment of the modern spirit of freedom, which was emerging, particularly in Florence, into the light of day with the weapons of thinking and art.[283]

There is no better example of how useful one-point, or centralized perspective and *stiacciato* could be to sculptors for suggesting space than Donatello's early bronze panel of the *Feast of Herod* also known as the *Dance of Salome*, executed in the mid-1420s. (Plate 37.)[284] This panel represents a high point in the creation of the illusion of space and also in intensity of narrative in early Renaissance relief sculpture. Rosa Maria Letts' description of this work of art could hardly be bettered:

> First of all the choice of the episode to illustrate the story could not be more dramatic. Herod's banquet and Salome's dance are interrupted by the sudden appearance of a soldier carrying the severed head of St John on a platter.

With every justification Donatello may be regarded as being the most significant creative artist of the quattrocento.[285] Heinrich Wölfflin wrote of him; 'He is a sculptor who looks at humanity, searching for the characteristic form even in the depths of ugliness, and who then, suddenly pure and serene, is able to express his vision of beauty, calm, noble and almost magical.'[286] Richard Turner[287] suggests that it is unlikely that the humanist Leon Battista Alberti, thinking about 'illusionistic space'[288] in his *Della Pittura* (*Treatise on Painting*) of 1435, sharply distinguished painting from pictorial relief sculpture. For instance, in Donatello's bronze relief of the *Feast of Herod* just mentioned the ground plane is not only visible, it is demarcated in a way which reveals the sculptor's use of the linear perspective developed by his contemporary, Brunelleschi. The complex architectural scheme is also controlled by the same formula.

Epilogue

As we have seen, the Italian Renaissance was an era whose focus was *man* and a time in which the increasing emphasis on man and on the worldly constituted a clear distinction from the beliefs of the Middle Ages and the doctrines of Christianity as perceived during those centuries. In contrast to the man of the Renaissance, whose interest clearly lies 'in the world of human experience,' the man of the Middle Ages 'believes his true life to be in another world', that is, in the afterlife, when united with God.[289] The ideal in the Middle Ages was the renunciation of all that was physical or worldly and concentration was focussed on God, not on man. During the years of transition, the years between the Middle Ages and the Italian Renaissance, men and women were torn between the seemingly exclusive ideas of the two ages. The humanists of the early Renaissance (e.g. the Florentine Academy) were the first to 'aspire towards the fusion of the two ideals hitherto irreconcilable; the classic ideal of beauty and the Christian ideal of moral perfection'.[290] Through this attempted 'fusion', the philosophy which gradually emerged and dominated the Italian Renaissance was Neoplatonism.

In 1438, learned Greeks came to Italy to attend the council of Ferrara and Florence. There were, in particular, two events which helped sow the seeds for the subsequent 'adoption' of Neoplatonism in Florence. Namely, one Greek philosopher, Pletho, befriended Cosimo de' Medici, encouraging him to establish Florence as the centre of the new Platonic Academy; and another Greek, Bessarion, who came to Italy and was 'reconciled to the Roman Church and raised to the cardinalate',[291] also had significant influence in Italy. In his book *In Calumniatorem Platonis*, printed in Rome in 1469, he clearly delineated the links between and similarities in Platonism and Christianity. These two Greeks, together with others, handed the Florentines the tools they needed in order to be able to realize their search for the fusion of pagan beauty and philosophy and Christian morality.[292]

All the States in Italy took part in the Renaissance movement. In the first half of the quattrocento, however, it was Florence that held the foremost place. Florence, in the fifteenth century, was a rich and prosperous city organized as an oligarchic republic. The Renaissance was clearly a crucial turning point in Western intellectual and cultural experience of both the *self* of man and the physical, natural world in which he lived. Man became conscious of himself, of his fellow human beings, and of his environment, in a way which, characteristic of the emerging consciousness soul, brought with it the capacity to separate oneself from the object—including one's individual self—under observation. Florentine art, architecture and thought decisively broke with the medieval world view, by embracing secular reason and emphasizing the human form and the natural world. Though clearly not anti-Christian, Renaissance men and women embraced the possibilities of life on earth rather than focusing on the hereafter. Further, instead of renouncing earthly endeavours for contemplation on God, emphasis emerged on the cultivation of individualism and the particular role and achievements of each individual human being. Freedom of thought and deed became of paramount importance. Here we may think, for example, of Pico's view regarding the dignity of man.

The Renaissance was a major turning point in history from the Middle Ages in just about every element of the life of the individual human being and of society as a whole in the western hemisphere as we know it today. Scientific thinking took place in the fifteenth century alongside the Neoplatonic philosophy represented in particular by the Florentine Platonic Academy. However, during the centuries which followed, it became ever clearer that man had lost his connection with the universal hierarchically-ordered spiritual world and that only sense-experience and the intellectual processes based on this gave him certainty.[293] It is, in particular, through the spiritual science given to humankind by Rudolf Steiner (1861–1925) that it is now becoming possible to regain, consciously, a living insight into and relationship with the creative working of the spiritual powers underlying the sense-perceptible world.

Notes and References

Key to Publishers
RSP = Rudolf Steiner Press, UK
AP/SB = SteinerBooks (Anthroposophic Press), USA

1. *A Miniature History of Music* (numerous editions), p. 9.
2. Quoted from the journal *Anthroposophy*, Vol. III. No. 7 (July 1924).
3. *The Living Tree, Art and the Sacred* (Green Books, 1988), p. 59.
4. The noun 'man' is used in the sense of either gender throughout this book.
5. Gary Lachman in his book *Rudolf Steiner. An Introduction to his Life and Work*, writes, 'Our task is the development of what Steiner called the "consciousness soul", whose mission is to combine the clear consciousness of the scientific mind with the vital awareness of the spiritual world present in our earlier incarnations.' (Floris Books, Edinburgh 2007), p. 147.
6. Op. cit., Mercury Press, (Spring Valley, New York, 1989), pp. 21–21.
7. *Shakespeare's Flowering of the Spirit* (The Lanthorn Press, 1971), p. 132. [My emphasis.]
8. See Brian Clegg, *The First Scientist, A Life of Roger Bacon* (Constable, 2003).
9. Gary Lachman, *A Secret History of Consciousness* (Lindisfarne Books, 2003), pp. 218–220.
10. From James Laver, 'The Cradle Of Venus' in *The Scallop: Studies of a Shell and its Influences on Humankind* (published in London by the Shell Transport and Trading Company Ltd, 1957) p. 73. The wording has been slightly changed.
11. Rudolf Steiner, *From Symptom to Reality in Modern History* (RSP, 1976).
12. In Part Two: The Development of the Individual.
13. Stewart Easton in his book *Man and World in the Light of Anthroposophy* comments: 'Throughout the entire epoch of the intellectual soul [from mid-eighth century BC to beginning of the fifteenth century AD] not many men or women did come to experience themselves as "I". Throughout this period the consciousness of being a member of a group was far stronger than the consciousness of being an individual. We shall call this pre-ego consciousness a "group soul" consciousness. Clearly enough it persists to the present day in most people of the world and, even in the West where on the whole consciousness has evolved the furthest, the feeling called "nationalism", an emotional awareness of belonging to a particular nation, may often lead to the complete submersion of the individuality, to say nothing of the forgetting of all awareness of being also a member of humanity' (p. 59).
14. Out of the spirit of independence parliamentary government developed in England.

15. The anger of his followers in Bohemia (Hussites) led to the Hussite Wars, which lasted until the mid-fifteenth century. See Renate Riemeck, *Glaube-Dogma-Macht. Geschichte der Konzilien*; also Walter Nigg, *The Heretics, Heresy through the Ages*, pp. 268–74.
16. Rudolf Steiner, *From Symptom to Reality in Modern History*, p. 54.
17. See the first lecture of the series published in English under the title *The Destinies of Individuals and of Nations*, 1 September 1914–6 July 1915 (RSP, 1986). This verse, together with the German original, can also be found in *Verses and Meditations* (RSP, 1972).
18. In our time, in the individual human being, the consciousness soul may be considered as free to begin its full development when he or she reaches the mid-thirties. See Rudolf Treichler, *Soulways, The Developing Soul-Life Phases, Thresholds and Biography*.
19. D.E. Faulkner Jones, *The English Spirit, A New Approach through the World Conception of Rudolf Steiner* (London, 1935) p. 14.
20. Robert Maynard Hutchins (b. 17 Jan 1899–d. 17 May 1977).
21. Op. cit. p. 156.
22. Rudolf Steiner, *The New Spirituality and the Christ Experience of the Twentieth Century*, 22 October 1920 (RSP/AP 1988), also Rudolf Steiner, *Social and Anti-Social Forces in the Human Being*, Berne, 12 December 1918 (Mercury Press, 1982).
23. See also 30 May 1924 *Karmic Relationships, Vol. II* (RSP, 1974).
24. It was not called *The Divine Comedy (Divina)* until the sixteenth century.
25. Arnold Freeman, *Who was Rudolf Steiner? What is Anthroposophy?*
26. Rudolf Steiner, Lecture 9, 1 June 1908 of the cycle *The Influence of Spiritual Beings upon Man* (AP 1961).
27. Owen Barfield, *Romanticism Comes of Age* (1944), pp. 99–102.
28. Friedrich Hiebel, *Shakespeare and the Awakening of Modern Consciousness.*
29. See, for instance, Rudolf Steiner, *The Study of Man* (RSP, 2004).
30. Re the need for 'living thinking' see, for instance, Stewart C. Easton, *Man and World in the Light of Anthroposophy* (AP, 1975), pp. 265–266; 269–278; 299–300; 332; 450–451.
31. See also Owen Barfield, *Saving the Appearances*; also Faulkner Jones, op. cit. p. 77
32. Gaia Servadio, *Renaissance Woman* (I.B. Taurus, 2005) p. 1.
33. See Paleotti, *Archiepiscopale Bononiense* (Rome, 1594), p. 81. Cited by Anthony Blunt, *Artistic Theory in Italy 1450–1600* (Oxford University Press, 1964), p. 78.
34. Lecture I, 8 October 1916.
35. Quoted from Gladys Mayer, *Sleeping and Waking and the Life of Art* (London, 1932).
36. See also Bishop Richard Harries' sensitive description of Fra Angelico's *Annunciation in A Gallery of Reflection. The Nativity of Christ* (Lion Publishing. The Bible Reading Fellowship, Oxford, 1995), pp. 20–21.

37. In the introduction to her book, *Masonry & Medieval Mysticism*, Isabel Cooper-Oakley writes: 'The Catholic Church permitted no education, no freedom of religious thought, and, knowing the unstable basis on which she stood, the Dominicans in the early Middle Ages took up the very simple position of entirely forbidding the reading of the Bible, except in such scamped versions as were authorized; and all who did not obey were removed by the Church. Indeed, the bloodiest and blackest records that history can show us are the attacks of the Catholic church on the mystics of all these centuries.

    "We do condemn to perpetual infamy the Cathari, the Patarines, the Leonists, the Speronists, . . . and all other heretics of both sexes by what name soever they are called. . . ." Thus thundered Pope Honorius III in the fourteenth century.' *Masonry and Medieval Mysticism* (Theosophical Publishing House Ltd., 1977. See also *History of the Christian Church*, by the Rev. Henry Stebbing, (London, 1834), ii. 301.
38. Faulkner Jones op. cit. pp. 14–5.
39. Ibid. p. 15.
40. As we have seen, one of the principal characteristics of the consciousness soul is that of objectivity, which results from the ability of the self to withdraw completely from the subject being studied. For this reason Rudolf Steiner also spoke of this soul as the 'spectator' soul.
41. Rudolf Steiner spoke on one occasion of the contrast between what he called 'head-life' and the life that expresses itself in the limb and metabolic system: 'The head represents the dying part of man's being, for the head is perpetually involved in death. Life is only possible because through the whole of earthly life, forces are continually pouring from the metabolic process to the head. If the head were to unfold merely its own natural forces, they would be the forces of death. But to this dying we owe the fact that we can think and be conscious beings. The moment the pure life-forces flow in excess to the head, consciousness is prone to be lost. Basically speaking, then, life makes for a *dimming* of consciousness; death pouring into life makes for a *lighting-up* of consciousness. If only very little of what is rightly located in the stomach, for example, were to pass up to the head, the head would be without consciousness—like the stomach.' From the lecture 'The Relationship of Man with the Cosmos' Oslo, 24 February 1921. See *Self-consciousness, The Spiritual Human Being* (Garber, Blauvelt USA, 1986).

    Bernhard Behrens in an essay with the title 'Aphorisms on Freedom' (in the quarterly journal *Proteus* (Summer 1951) wrote: 'Processes of consciousness do not aid the life-processes active in matter; they obstruct them. They are inimical to the life-processes active in the metabolism, which are unconscious. One becomes conscious of life processes only when the disease of an organ disturbs their normal activity. A disturbance is experienced as pain and is thus brought to consciousness. Our sense-functions are centralized in the brain. The nerve-substances are engendered and built up by the metabolism during sleep—that is, during the unconscious period of existence. When, during perception, the senses are consciously active in connection with the thought-processes, the nerve-substances disintegrate; and they are built up again and supplemented, materially, by forces from the sphere of the unconscious life.

42. It struck Europe (1347–50) and returned intermittently until 1383.
43. See Alice K. Turner *The History of Hell* (Harcourt Brace & Co., 1993), pp. 123–26.
44. Francis Edmunds, *Anthroposophy, A Way of Life* (Carnant Books, 1982) pp. 126–8.
45. The first lecture of a series Rudolf Steiner gave on the History of Art: *Kunstgeschichte als Abbild innerer geistiger Impulse*, GA 292, 8 October 1916.
46. See previous note.
47. J.V. Field, *The Invention of Infinity, Mathematics and Art in the Renaissance*; also Field's essay 'Masaccio and Perspective in Italy in the Fifteenth Century' in *The Cambridge Companion to Masaccio*. Edited by Diane Cole Ahl.
48. B.J. Nesfield-Cookson, *Rudolf Steiner's Vision of the Power of Love*. (Sophia Books, RSP, 1999.)
49. It is not to be wondered at that the invented art of printing was initially not welcomed by the wealthy collectors of manuscripts because it depreciated the value of their collection.
50. Emperor of Byzantium 1425–1448.
51. Pope 1431–1447.
52. In the fifth lecture of the cycle *Gegenwärtiges und Vergangenes im Menschengeiste*, GA 167, 11 April 1916.
53. Those who believe that the Christian revelation has a humanistic emphasis point to the fact that man was made in the image of God; that Jesus Christ became man through the incarnation, and that the worth of the individual is a consistent theme in the teaching of Christ. Indeed, in St Matthew's Gospel we hear that Christ exhorted those who listened to him to 'Love the Lord your god with all your heart, and with all your soul, and with all your mind' and to 'love your neighbour as yourself' (22:37, 39).
54. See also J.R. Hale, *England and the Italian Renaissance* (Faber & Faber Ltd, 1954).

    In the late 1480s, early 1490s, Erasmus was already reacting against scholasticism and was drawn to the humanists. He became strongly critical of the pedantries and abuses of the Catholic Church, and his *Colloquia Familaria* of 1518 helped prepare the way for Martin Luther and the Reformation.
55. Rudolf Steiner continues: '[Sir Thomas More] it was who wrote *Utopia*, a wonderful work in which, out of a kind of visionary perception, he created the idea of a social relationship among men.' See lecture seven (1 October 1916) in *Inner Impulses of Evolution* (AP, 1984), p. 136.

In her comprehensive study *The French Academies of the Sixteenth Century*, Frances A. Yates shows how Florentine Neoplatonism, with its aim of reconciling not only philosophy and religion but religious factions and religions themselves, had pronounced influence on the development of the Academies. (Routledge, 1988). Elsewhere Frances Yates gives us a picture of the French scholar, Louis Le Roy's work, which included the translation into French of some of the major works of Plato, with commentaries, and of the *Politics* of Aristotle. Le Roy's translations and commentaries were an important factor in spreading knowledge of the Renaissance revival of Plato and the Neoplatonist in France, since he used in his commentaries the works of Italian philosophers, particularly those of Ficino and Pico. *Ideas and Ideals in the North European Renaissance*. Collected essays, Vol. III (Routledge & Kegan Paul, 1984), p. 135.

56. See Peter J. French, *John Dee, The World of the Elizabethan Magus* (Routledge & Kegan Paul, 1972).
57. And both were also profoundly affected by the German continuers of the movement, particularly by Henry Cornelius. See Frances A. Yates, *Lull & Bruno*. Collected essays, Vol. 1 (Routledge & Kegan Paul, 1982), p. 210. See also Désirée Hirst, *Hidden Riches, Traditional Symbolism from the Renaissance to Blake*, regarding Cornelius Agrippa and his controversial volume, the *De Occulta Philosophia* (Eyre & Spottiswoode, 1964), Ch. II.
58. See C.S. Lewis, *Spenser's Images of Life* (Ed. Alastair Fowler, Cambridge University Press, 1967), pp. 8–9.

    In her deeply researched book *The French Academies of the Sixteenth Century*, Frances A. Yates shows in some detail how Florentine Neoplatonism, with its aim of reconciling not only philosophy and religion but religious factions and religions themselves, was transmitted to France by intermediaries such as Maurice Scève and Marguerite de Navarre. (Routledge, 1988).
59. Jill Line, *Shakespeare and the Fire of Love* (Shepherd-Walwyn Ltd, 2004). Ch. 1.
60. First published in 1947 by the Warburg Institute. See note 55 above.
61. It should be noted here, in passing, that many Christians, including the reformer Girolamo (1452–98) and the Swiss religious reformer Ulrich Zwingli (1484–1531), reacted strongly against the secular approach of Humanism.
62. See J.H. Plumb, *The Penguin Book of The Renaissance* (Penguin Books, 1964), p. 263.
63. Vincent Cronin, *The Florentine Renaissance* (Collins, 1967), p. 137.
64. Gerhard Dohrn van Rossum, *Die Geschichte der Stunde: Uhren und moderne Zeitordnungen* (Carl Hanser Verlag, München 1992).
65. Ibid. p. 144.
66. Ibid.
67. *The Letters of Marsilio Ficino*, Vol. 1, (Shepheard-Walwyn, 1975), letter 42, p. 84.

68. See P.O. Kristeller, *Renaissance Concepts of Man*, ch. 2.
69. Ibid.
70. See http://easyweb.easynet.co.uk/-opheus/ficino.htm; also some of Ficino's letters to Lorenzo de' Medici in *The Letters of Marsilio*. Vols I to VII. First published, in English translation, by Shepheard-Walwyn Ltd., London, 1975 onwards.
71. Panofsky, op. cit., p. 141.
72. Gerardus van der Leeuw, *Sacred and Profane: the Holy in Art* (Holt, Rinehart and Winston, Inc., USA 1963).
73. Pietro Fachetti's contemporary copy of the lost work by the early Renaissance artist Pinturicchio (Bernardino di Betto, c.1454–1513), painted for the Borgia apartments in the Vatican, showed the Borgia Pope Alexander VI kneeling at the feet of the Madonna and child and cradling the infant Jesus's right foot in his left hand. It was an open secret at the court that the 'Madonna' was Giulia Farnese, the 60-year Pope's beautiful young married mistress. (Reported in *The Times* 21 June 2006.)
74. Vincent Cronin, *The Florentine Renaissance* (Collins, 1967), p. 189.
75. See note 62.
76. Hence the title of Fra Luca Pacioli's architectural treatise, *Divina Proportione*. A work for which Leonardo da Vinci illustrated the Vitruvian concept of a man circumscribed by a square and a circle.
77. See C.Warren Hollister, M.Judith Bennett: *Medieval Europe, a Short History* (2002, 9th edition), pp. 329–333.
78. See Peter J. Gärtner, *Brunelleschi* (Könemann Verlagsgesellschaft, 1998) pp. 14–19.
79. Giorgio Vasari (1511–74). Italian architect and painter, but best known for his *Vite de' piu eccellenti Pittori, Scultori e Archittori* (1550, *Lives of the Most Excellent Painters, Sculptors and Architects*), a book of biographies and of art criticism.
80. See Rudolf Steiner's first lecture in the cycle *The Gospel of St Mark* (AP, 1986).
81. See note 86, op. cit. p. 133.
82. See also A. C. Harwood, *Shakespeare's Prophetic Mind* (RSP, 1964), p. 34.
83. The German artist Albrecht Dürer (1471–1528) created a remarkable series of landscape watercolours as a consequence of his Italian journeys.
84. *De ente et uno*, V. Quoted in Martin Kemp, *Leonardo da Vinci, The Marvellous Works of Nature and Man* (J.M. Dent & Sons, 1989), p. 128.
85. Leonardo da Vinci, *Treatise on Painting* (Codex Urbinas Latinus 1270), ed. A.P. McMahon, 2 vols (Princeton, 1956.) Urb.iv.
86. As note 84, Urb. 19r. See also Kenneth Clark, *Leonardo da Vinci* Ch. 2, 1481–1490.
87. *Art and Human Consciousness* (Floris Books, 1985).
88. Part I, Scene IV, ll. 407–410 (tr. Bayard Taylor).
89. See note 23.

90. *The Dignity of Man* (Harper Brothers, New York, 1955), p. 231.
91. Quoted by W.R. Inge in a paper entitled 'Plotinus' he read for the British Academy on 30 January 1929. See *Mysticism in Religion* (Rider & Co., 1969), pp. 138–158.
92. In the early 1460s, Cosimo also built and furnished a convent library at the Badia in Fiesole overlooking Florence. His first library was a gift in return for Venetian hospitality and goodwill. Thankful for the shelter provided during a short exile, Cosimo built and furnished in 1433 a library for the San Giorgio Maggiore monastery in Venice.
93. Tim Parks, *Medici Money. Banking, Metaphysics, and Art in Fifteenth Century Florence* (W.W. Norton & Co., 2005), p. 124.
94. *Cosimo de'Medici and the Florentine Renaissance: The Patron's Oeuvre* (New Haven and London: Yale University Press, 2000), p. 178.

    Niccolò de'Niccoli (1364–1437), was born and died in Florence, and was one of the principal figures in the company of learned men which gathered round Cosimo de'Medici.
95. Robert J. Clements, *Michelangelo's Theory of Art* (New York University Press, 1961), p. 16.
96. *Per fido esemplo alla mia vocazione/ Nel part mi fu data la bellezza,/ Che d'ambo l'arti m'è lucerna e specchio:/ S'altro si pensa è falsa opinione. / Questo sol l'occhio porta a quella altezza, / Ch'a pingere e scolpir qui m'apparecchio.*
97. See, for instance, Chapters 1 and 2 in Anthony Blunt's *Artistic Theory in Italy 1450–1600* (Oxford University Press, 1964).
98. See Martin Kemp, *Leonardo da Vinci, The Marvellous Works of Nature and Man* (J.M. Dent & Sons Ltd, London,1989), p. 91.
99. See http://www.historyguide.org/intellect/ren_res.html.
100. See the lecture Rudolf Steiner gave on 16 September 1916, *The Inner Impulses of Evolution* (AP, 1984).
101. Frank Avray Wilson, *Art's Revelation* (Centaur Press, 1981), p. 245.
102. By the late fourteenth century, the term 'humanitatis' ('humanistic studies') had come to mean a well-defined cycle of education, including the study of grammar, rhetoric, history, poetry, and moral philosophy.
103. It was from the fifteenth century Italian *umanista*, the man who used the classical texts to teach the *literae humaniores*, the branches of study most concerned with the secular condition (grammar and eloquence, history, poetry and moral philosophy), that the word 'humanism' was created in the nineteenth century to describe the conditioning of ideas that drew on a knowledge of classical antiquity. In c.1402 Pietro Paolo Vergerio wrote his manifesto of liberal education *On the Conduct of Honourable Men*. While the body was to be kept fit by exercise, lessons were to shape the pupil's character and prepare him for a life of useful service. Grammar was to enable him to master the exemplary texts that would make his speech and writing easy and adaptable to different subjects and groups of people. History would provide him with the virtues of the heroes of epic literature.

Moral philosophy aimed to stress the high standards of personal behaviour. See John Hale, *The Civilization of Europe in the Renaissance*. Slightly adapted, p. 194 in 1993 edition (Harper Collins).

104. First published by Nisbet & Co. Ltd. 1952, in chapter 'Being and Courage'.
105. Rudolf Steiner, *The Mission of Folk-Souls* (RSP, 1970), Lecture 6, 12 June 1910.
106. See Jenifer Capper's essay on Dean Colet in the collection of essays by various authors published under the title *Friend to Mankind: Marsilio Ficino* (ed. Michael Shepherd, Shepheard-Walwyn Ltd; 1999).
107. See also J.R. Hale, *England and the Italian Renaissance* (Faber & Faber Ltd, 1954).

    In the late 1480s, early 1490s, Erasmus was already reacting against scholasticism and was drawn to the humanists. He became strongly critical of the pedantries and abuses of the Catholic Church, and his *Colloquia Familaria* of 1518 helped prepare the way for Martin Luther and the Reformation.
108. 1500 and later editions.
109. See Lecture VII in the cycle of lectures mentioned in note 100 above.
110. *The Platonic Renaissance in England*, trans. James P. Pettegrove (Nelson, 1955), p. 25.
111. *The Seventeenth Century Background* (Penguin Books, 1962), p. 126.
112. See Peter Milward, *Shakespeare's Religious Background* (Sidgwick & Jackson, 1973). In particular Ch. X, 'Elizabethan Atheisim'.
113. Ibid. p. 201.
114. *The Letters of Marsilio Ficino* Vol. 1, Letter 7, p. 45.
115. *The Merchant of Venice* V.1.55–65.
116. See note 112, pp. 45–46.
117. Ibid.
118. In the Icon Edition, Harper & Row, 1972. Footnote p. 138. See also bibliography p. 248 reference 355 in this edition.
119. Faber & Faber, 1958, Ch. 7.
120. Frank Avray Wilson, *Art's Revelation* (Centaur Press Ltd, 1981), p. 142.
121. C.C. Martindale, *The Religion of Ancient Greece* (London 1943), p. 11.
122. Rudolf Steiner, *Isis. Mary. Sophia*, selected lectures and writings (SB, 2003); Emil Bock, *Threefold Mary* (SB, 2003). Also Dora Baker 'Lorenzo de'Medici and the Platonic Academy in Florence', in Anthroposophic News Sheet, Vol. 26, Nos. 35/36, September 1958.
123. Rudolf Steiner's lecture of 24 May 1912, *The Meaning of Life* (RSP, 1999).
124. Philip Sherrard in *Human Image: World Image. The Death and Resurrection of Sacred Cosmology* (Golgonooza Press, Ipswich, 1992), discusses this in some detail.
125. Published in *Renaissance Thought and the Arts; Collected Essays.*
126. My emphases.
127. Hermes Trismegistus is the Greek name for the Egyptian god Thoth,

identified with the Greek Hermes. The Neoplatonists attributed the hermetic books, works containing the collected occult knowledge of ancient Egypt to him. In the Alexandrian writings attributed to Hermes Trismegistus, the *Asclepius* and the *Pimander*—which Ficino had translated in 1463, Pico would have read that while the stars do affect man's physical body they have no influence over his mind.

128. Quoted in E. Cassirer, P.O. Kristeller and J.H. Randall (eds); *The Renaissance Philosophy of Man* (Chicago and London, 1948), pp. 224–5. See also Erwin Panofsky, *Studies in Iconology, Humanistic Themes in the Art of the Renaissance* (Icon Edition, Harper & Row, 1972), pp. 134–35.
129. Richard Hooker http://www.wsu.edu:8080/-dee/REN/PICO.HTM
130. Marsilio Ficino, *Commentary on Plato's Symposium on Love*, trans. Sears Jayne, Spring Publications, Dallas, 1985, p. 134.
131. Jill Line, *Shakespeare and the Fire of Love* (Shepheard-Walwyn Ltd. 2004), p. 162. See also Frances A. Yates, *Shakespeare's Last Plays, A New Approach* (Routledge & Kegan Paul, 1975).
132. RSP, 1970, p. 158.
133. In the *Heptaplus*.
134. See comment made in the chapter 'The Academy in Florence' that a synthesis of Platonism and Aristotelianism was not achieved.
135. Cronin op. cit. pp. 142–43.
136. *The Letters of Marsilio Ficino*, Vol.1, (Shepheard-Walwyn, 1975), letter 42, p. 84.
137. It has been translated into English by Sears Jayne with the title *Commentary on Plato's Symposium on Love*.
138. Quoted by Sears Jayne. See notes 63.
139. Icon editions, Harper & Row, 1972, pp. 131–140.
140. Ibid. ch. 2, p. 30 seq.
141. P.O. Kristeller, *Renaissance Thoughts and the Arts* (Princeton University Press, 1990) p. 108.
142. See *www.Theosophy.Org.Theosophy* Library Online. Great Teacher Series. For the Florentine Neoplatonists it was a matter of course to connect the Platonic idea of pre-existence and reincarnation with the dogma of resurrection in the Christian sense. See Erwin Panofsky, *Studies in Iconology* (Icon Editions, Harper & Row, 1972), p.138, footnote 29a.
143. Ficino's essay *De Christiana Religione* appeared in the mid 1470s and was dedicated to Lorenzo de'Medici.
144. Letter to Filippo Controni, see Erwin Panofsky, *Studies in Iconology, Humanistic Themes in the Art of the Renaissance* (Icon Editions. Harper & Row, 1972), pp. 140–41.
145. Quoted, in Latin, by Panofsky, op. cit. p. 217.
146. Quoted, in Latin and Italian, by Panofsky, op. cit. footnote p. 141.
147. P.O. Kristeller, *Renaissance Thought and the Arts*. See note 57.
148. Marsilio Ficino, *Commentary on Plato's Symposium on Love*. An English

translation by Sears Jayne. (Spring Publications Inc., Dallas, Texas 1985), Speech II, Chapter 8, p. 54.

149. A metaphor of the tomb representing the symbolic confines of the soul in the terrestrial world is found in Plato's *Cratylus*.
150. D.P. Walker, *The Ancient Theology*. Introduction (Ithaca: Cornell University Press 1972), p. 59.
151. Frances A.Yates, *Giordano Bruno and the Hermetic Tradition* (Routledge and Kegan Paul, 1964, 1971) p. 117. See also the whole of chapter VI.
152. To date (2008) seven volumes have been translated into English by members of the Language Department of the School of Economic Science, London.
153. P. O. Kristeller, *The Philosophy of Marsilio Ficino* (New York 1943, 1964), and *Studies in Renaissance Thought and Letters* (Rome 1956, 1969).
154. June Davie's Review of *The Letters of Marsilio Ficino* Vol. 1 (Shepheard-Walwyn 1975) in *The Christian Community Journal*, No. 1, January–February, 1976.
155. Phidias was a Greek sculptor appointed by Pericles (c.495–429 BC), the ruler of Athens from c.460 until his death, to beautify Athens. His works include the sculptural decorations of the Parthenon and the monumental statue of the Greek goddess of wisdom and the arts and handicrafts, Athena, which the temple housed, as well as the statue of her father Zeus at Olympia.
156. Kenneth Clark, *Civilisation*, pp. 94–5.
157. Georges Duby, *The Age of the Cathedrals, Art and Society, 980–1420* (Croom Helm, 1981), p. 196. Translated by Eleanor Levieux and Barbara Thompson from the French edition, *Le Temps des Cathedrals: L'Art et la Société 980–1420*, 1976.
158. See previous note. Op. cit. p. 274.
159. Real name: Donato di Niccolò.
160. The German artist Albrecht Dürer (1471–1528) signed his work with the initials AD.
161. An illusionary effect of reality produced e.g. by shading and perspective.
162. L.B. Alberti, architect, was born in Genoa, but worked in Florence from 1428 and became one of the best-known figures of the Renaissance. His *Della Pittura* (1435–6) contains the first description of perspective construction. His own designs, which include the churches of San Francesco in Rimini and Santa Maria Novella in Florence, are among the best examples of the pure classical style.
163. L.B. Alberti, *Opera Inedita* (Florence 1890), p. 293.

     Jacob Burckhardt in his book *The Civilisation of the Renaissance in Italy* (translated into English in 1878 by S.G.C. Middlemore) wrote of Alberti, after claiming him to be an 'all-sided' man, a Renaissance man: 'He learned music without a master, and yet his compositions were admired by professional judges. Under the pressure of poverty, he studied both civil and canonical law for many years, till exhaustion brought on a severe illness. In his twenty-fourth year, finding his memory for words weakened, but his sense of facts unimpaired, he set to work at physics and mathematics. And all the while he acquired every sort of accomplishment and dexterity, cross-examining artists, scholars and artisans of all descriptions, down to the cobblers, about the secrets and peculiarities of their craft. Painting and modelling he practised by the way, and especially excelled in admirable likeness from memory. Great admiration was excited by his mysterious "camera obscura", in which he showed at one time the stars and the moon rising over rocky hills, ... And that which others created he welcomed joyfully, and held every *human achievement* [my emphasis] which followed the laws of beauty, for something almost divine. To all this must be added his literary works, first of all those on art, which are landmarks and authorities of the first order for the Renaissance of form, especially in architecture; then his Latin prose writings, ... And all that he had and knew he imparted, as rich natures always do, without the least reserve, giving away his chief discoveries for nothing. But the deepest spring of his nature has yet to be spoken of—the sympathetic intensity with which he entered into the whole life around him. At the sight of noble trees and waving cornfields he shed tears, handsome and dignified old men he honoured as "a delight of nature", and could never look at them enough. Perfectly formed animals won his good will as being specially favoured by nature, and more than once, when he was ill, the sight of a beautiful landscape cured him. ... It need not be added that an iron will pervaded and sustained his whole personality, like all the great men of the Renaissance, he said, "*Men can do all things if they will*"' (my emphasis).

164. Benvenuto Cellini, (1500–71), goldsmith, sculptor and engraver.
165. The actual fall of Florence came quickly. In 1529 the Prince of Orange lay siege to the city with a powerful army. In August 1530 Florence fell, immediately lost her independence, and had to accept a long line of dukes nominated by the Emperor Charles V. Her decline, which had begun in 1494, became even more pronounced, for the basis of her major achievements had been freedom.
166. H. Caudwell, *The Creative Impulse in Writing and Painting* (Macmillan & Co. Ltd, 1953), p. 144.
167. See Caudwell, op. cit., pp. 62–63.
168. 1593–1633. Metaphysical poet and clergyman.
169. See Nigel Pennick, *Sacred Geometry* (Turnstone Press, 1980), Ch. 7.
170. See Vol. I of Leonardo's Notebooks , p. 204. Arranged, rendered into English and introduced by Edward MacCurdy (The Reprint Society, 1954), p. 204. Also *Encyclopaedia of Modern Architecture*, General editor: Gerd Hatje (Thames and Hudson, 1963), p. 220.
171. In his treatise *De Architectura.*
172. *Liturgy and Architecture* (Barrie and Rockliff, 1960), p. 59.

173. Rudolf Wittkower, *Architectural Principles in the Age of Humanism* (Alec Tirani Ltd., 1962), p. 27.
174. *The Ten Books on Architecture*, Book III, Chapter 1.
175. 'A Review of Proportion' in *Module, Symmetry, Proportion* (Ed. Gyorgy Kepes, Studio Vista, 1966) p. 220.
176. Joseph Chiari, *Art and Knowledge* (Paul Elek, 1977), p. 84.
177. Printed in the collection *The Arts and their Mission* (AP, 1964).
178. J.H. Plumb, *The Penguin Book of the Renaissance* (Penguin Books 1964), p. 86.
179. *The Story of Art*, p. 169.
180. John Hale, op. cit. p. 256.
181. See E.H. Gombrich, *The Story of Art*, p. 170, see also Gärtner, op. cit. pp. 68–77.
182. The façade of this complex to house the children uses slender Corinthian columns to support round arches and a simple horizontal entablature. The cornice serves as a base for a row of windows with classically inspired pediments, one centred above each arch. It should be noted that rational and clear proportions are used throughout. The distance between the columns is the same as the distance from the columns to the wall. The distance between the floor of the loggia to just above the impost blocks is the same. Thus the cube is a major module in this proportional design. Other geometrical relationships govern the location of the cornice, the width of the doors and the heights of windows.
183. See David Mayernik, *Timeless Cities, An Architect's Reflections on Renaissance Italy* (Westview Press, 2003), p. 162.
184. See pp. 189 and 191 (slightly adapted). (Published by Libreria Editrice, Florence, 1962.)
185. Architectural sculpture is a general categorization used to describe items used for the decoration of buildings and structure. The term encompasses both sculpture that is attached to a building and free-standing pieces that are a part of the architects' design.
186. Lecture nine in a series of twelve on *Colour*, 2 June 1923.
187. See Margaret Bennell, *Shakespeare's Flowering of the Spirit* (Lanthorn Press, 1971), p. 132.
188. See endnote 112, pp. 22–25.
189. See William M. Ivins, *Art & Geometry* (Dover Publications, Inc. 1964).
190. *Roman Art and Architecture* (Thames and Hudson, 1964), p. 186.
191. Quoted by Hans-Werner Schroeder in an article he wrote in 1993. Published in the Christian Community Journal 'Perspectives', June 1993. See: Fred Gettings, *The Hidden Art, A study of occult symbolism in art* (Studio Vista, 1978), 127ff.; Dennis Sharp, *Modern Architecture and Expressionism* (Longmans, 1966), Ch. 1, 'The Dionysian Element', pp 3–18; Robert Rosenblum, *Modern Painting and the Northern Romantic Tradition* (Thames and Hudson, 1975; in particular Parts III an IV.; also *Towards a New Art.*

Essays on the Background to Abstract Art 1910–20 (Tate Gallery Publications, 1980).

192. Cupitt then makes the perceptive statement: 'Van Eyck can do both, indeed, he can sometimes show us the two versions side by side in the same work. When he paints a theological topic, van Eyck is producing a representation of a universal theme, and doing so according to canonical rules, but when he paints a patron, or some other man or woman, he is *freed from the universal, free to be just one individual mortal* looking at another, free to show that the human eye is more merciful than God' [my emphases]. *After God, The Future of Religion* (Weidenfeld & Nicolson, 1997), p. 64.
193. Letts, op. cit. p. 38.
194. J. Brotton, 'Science and Philosophy', *The Renaissance: A Very Short Introduction* (Oxford University Press, 2006).
195. J. Brotton, in his *Short Introduction*, mentions that with the publication of Vesalius's *De Humani Corporis Fabrica* ('On the Structure of the Human Body'), in 1543, a new confidence was placed in the role of dissection, observation, and a mechanistic view of anatomy.
196. P. 159. The work by H.G. Evers to which Gerardus van der Leeuw refers is *Staat aus dem Stein* (Munich, 1929).
197. c.580–c.500 BC.
198. Her article *The Renaissance Mind Mirrored in Art*. Published in the Magazine; *World and I*. Vol. 13. Issue 12, December 1998.
199. Ibid.
200. Ibid.
201. Erwin Panofsky, *Perspective as Symbolic Form*, translated by Christopher S. Wood. (MIT Press, USA, 1993).
202. John Lane, *The Living Tree, Art and the Sacred* (Green Books, 1988), p. 30.
203. Letts, op. cit. p. 51.
204. Art responds to the Bible (Pendle hill Pamphlet 197, Oct. 1974), p. 4.
205. Underweysung der Messung (Nuremberg, 1525). Translated into English by E.H. Gombrich; see pp. 112–13 in his book *The Heritage of Apelles, Studies in the Art of the Renaissance* (Phaidon Press, 1976).
206. Ibid. p. 113.
207. See http://www.kijasto.sci.fi/Alberti.htm, p. 2. After Alberti, Piero della Francesca presented his own theory of perspective in *Se Prospective Pingandi*.
208. Without going into detail here, the other eight forms are: five regular polygons (the square, hexagon, octagon, decagon and dodecagon) and three rectangles (the square and a half, square and a third and a double square).
209. Only three round temples survived from Classical times: the Pantheon and the small temples at Tivoli and Rome.
210. E.g. the Temple Church, London; church of the Holy Sepulchre at Cambridge and at Northampton, and the ruined chapel of Ludlow Castle. [The last three are not confirmed as Templar churches, Ed.] See Cope, Gilbert *Symbolism in the Bible and the Church* (SCM Press 1959).

211. Nigel Pennick, *Sacred Geometry*, p. 116. See also E. Baldwin Smith, *The Dome, A Study in the History of Ideas* (Princeton University Press,1971), e.g. pp. 98–100.
212. See the eighth lecture, given 24 November 1921, of the cycle *Self-Consciousness, The Spiritual Human Being*.
213. Rudolf Wittkower, in a footnote on page 29 of the 1962 edition of his book *Architectural Principles in the Age of Humanism* comments: 'There seems to be little doubt that the wholesale acceptance of the Greek Cross as a plan for churches belongs to the history of the Greek 'invasion' of Italy during the fifteenth century'.
214. Ibid. p. 30.
215. The Italian High Renaissance architect Andrea Palladio (1508–80) was one of the greatest exponents of 'sacred' geometry. In his influential work *Quattro Libri dell'Architettura* (Isaac Ware, tr. *The Four books of Andrea Palladio's Architecture*, 1738) he stressed his debt to Vitruvius and also to Alberti. However, it was to the former that he owed his greatest inspiration. The Palladian style was widely imitated all over Europe, in particular by Inigo Jones and Christopher Wren.
216. See lecture seven in *The Festivals and their Meaning*. Easter, 10 April 1909.
217. See lecture of 9 March 1910 'Correlations between the Microcosm and the Macrocosm' in the cycle *The Christ Impulse and the Development of Ego Consciousness* (AP, 1976).

   See also: *Foundations of Esotericism*. Lecture 28, 31 October 1905 (RSP, 1983); *Wonders of the World* (RSP, 1983); Lecture 20 August 1911; *Macrocosm and Microcosm*, 11 lectures, 21–31 March 1910 (RSP, 1968).
218. In Part Four, 'The discovery of the world and of man'.
219. See Paul M. Allen, and Joan deRis Allen, *Francis of Assisi's* Canticle of the Creatures (Floris Books, 1996). Also Rudolf Steiner, *The Spiritual Foundation of Morality. Francis of Assisi and the Christ Impulse* (AP, 1995).
220. 'Nature first appears in the form of clearly defined objects: thus in Egyptian wall-painting we see the papyrus plants of the Nile delta, each plant carefully outlined. Water, obviously a more difficult problem, is rendered by a sort of shorthand or symbolism in a series of wavy lines. For long ages thereafter, landscape was treated in an elementary way (though the Greek painters had some idea of space and there are scenes illustrating the Odyssey ... which show a perspective of rocks and a distant horizon).' William Gaunt, *The Observer's Book of Painting and Graphic Art* (Frederick Warne & Co. Ltd., 1964), pp. 56–57. See also *Landscape Painting from Giotto to Turner* by C. Lewis Hind (Chapman and Hall, 1923), pp. 51–55 and ch. IX.
221. Hubert van Eyck (c.1366–1426); Jan van Eyck (1390–1441).
222. *Leonardo da Vinci. The Marvellous Works of Nature and Man*, p. 128.
223. See: http.//www.liu.edu/cwis/CWP/library/sc/turinmilan/turinmilan.htm.
224. 14th edition, 1984.
225. Book ix, chap. 4.

226. Gombrich points out in a note that, in view of the importance of the text he gives the passage from the edition of 1486.
227. See Herbert Read, *Education through Art* (Faber and Faber. Numerous reprints), p. 63.
228. *The Republic*, III. See Read, op. cit., p. 63.
229. Letts p.20.
230. Ibid. p. 22.
231. Gottfried Richter, *Art and Human Consciousness* (Floris Books, 1985), pp. 168–9.
232. *The Visionary Eye* (MIT Press, 1978), pp. 143–44.
233. The National Gallery in London has excellent examples. First discovered in 1820 in Egyptian tombs; the work of Greek artists of the first four centuries AD.
234. William Gaunt, op. cit. p. 86. See also John Ferguson, *The Heritage of Hellenism* (Thames and Hudson, 1973), pp. 121–124.
235. See John Ferguson, *The Heritage of Hellenism* (Thames and Hudson, 1973), pp. 121–125. Regarding Biography, see pp. 100 and 124.
236. Ibid.
237. Rab Hatfield, *Botticelli's Uffizi 'Adoration', A Study in Pictorial Content.* (Princeton University Press, New Jersey, 1976), p. 83. See Ch. III and Plates 16–50.
238. Ficino, *Letters*, Vol 1, letter 38, to Giovanni Cavalcanti.
239. *Friend to Mankind*, 'Ficino and Portraiture', (Shepheard-Walwyn Ltd, 1999), p. 101.
240. Eugene Fromentin, *The Masters of Past Times. Dutch and Flemish Painting from Van Eyck to Rembrandt* (Phaidon, 1981), p. 236.
241. Kenneth Clark, *Civilisation* (John Murray, 2005), p. 104.
242. Referring to art in England, O. Elfrieda Saunders in her book *A History of English Art in the Middle Ages* comments that in the fourteenth century there was a new interest in naturalistic detail. 'Generalization and stylized renderings no longer satisfied in art; the form of birds, of leaves, or of human features was carefully imitated. An English Gothic artist's sketches of birds and animals are preserved to us in a manuscript of the Pepysian Library at Magdalene College, Cambridge, and show an astonishing familiarity with the forms of nature. But these touches of real observation were for the most part confined to detail, and did not in England and the other northern countries, as they did in Italy, form part of a general movement towards a new truth in art.' Pp. 110–12.
243. Philppino Lippi. Executed the figure of the son of Theophilus.
244. Whether, in fact, they were related is not known.
245. Thyssen-Bornemisza Collection, Madrid.
246. See Andreas Quermann, *Ghirlandaio* (Könemann Verlagsgesellschaft, 1998) for a more detailed description of this outstanding portrait.
247. See *The Lives of the Artists*, translated from the Italian by Julia Conaway Bondanella and Peter Bondanella, Oxford 1991.

248. See Andreas Quermann, *Ghirlandaio*, pp. 96, 130 and 132.
249. *The Letters of Marsilio Ficino*, Vol. 3, pp. 133–148.
250. Antonio Rossellino (1427–79).
251. See John Pope-Hennessy, *Italian Renaissance Sculpture* (Phaidon, 1985), p. 47; Plate 59.
252. Ibid. p. 51. The bust is now in the Bargello.
253. Re portraits also see E.H. Gombrich *The Heritage of Apelles* (Phaidon Press, 1976). In particular: 69f., 94f., 132f.
254. Active as a merchant of fine books, Vespasiano also aided Cosimo the Elder de'Medici in the creation of the Laurentian Library, and Federico da Montefeltro, the Duke of Urbino, in the collection of his library.
255. Xenophone, *Memorablia*, c.355–4 BC.
256. Andre Malraux, *The Metamorphosis of the Gods* (Secker and Warburg, 1960), pp. 392–93.
257. Ibid. p. 337.
258. In *Italian Painters of the Renaissance*.
259. See E.H. Gombrich, *New Light on Old Masters, Studies in the Art of the Renaissance* Vol. IV (Phaidon, Oxford, 1986). In the chapter entitled 'Ideal and Type in Italian Renaissance Painting' Gombrich discusses the rendering of the human head from the Byzantine type of the Virgin with the slanting, half-closed eyes through, in particular, to Raphael.
260. *Doors of Perception—Icons and their Spiritual Significance* (Mowbray, 1987), p. 55.
261. Giuseppe Flavo, Paul Grendler, ed. 'Matteo Palmieri' in *Encyclopedia of the Renaissance*, 1999, vol. 3, pp. 376–377.
262. According to Guglielmo Amerighi. See *The City of Florence* (Libreria Editrice Fiorentina n.d.), p. 110.
263. Giulio Carlo Argan, *Le Quinzième Siècle* (Skira, Geneva, 1955), p. 87.
264. Heinrich Wölfflin, *Classic Art* (Phaidon, 1986), p. 5.
265. He used a grid framework, tooled right into the surface, and very rigorous linear perspective. Even the nails are shown in perspective!
266. Quoted by Gärtner op. cit. p. 26, from Wolfgang Braunfels, *Brunelleschi und die Kirchenbaukunst des frühen Humanismus* (Basel and Frankfurt, 1981).
267. Loc. cit.
268. Another typical example can be seen in *The Creation of the World and the Expulsion from Paradise*, 1445, by the Sienese artist Giovanni di Paolo (c.1400–1482).
269. On the different styles of the two artists, see R. Longhi, *Fattidi Masolino e di Masaccio*, Critica d'Arte, XXV–XXVI, 1940. See also also Diane Cole Ahl, 'Masaccio in the Brancacci Chapel' in *The Cambridge Companion to Masaccio* (ed. Diana Cole Ahl, 2002).
270. Ibid. p. 178.
271. The sculptors were 'a half step ahead' of the painters in delineating the new language of forms. Donatello's David is one of his earliest works in marble

and was made more than a decade before the painters displayed a similar understanding of and respect for the human figure.

272. His full name was Donato di Niccolò di Betto Bardi.
273. H.D. Molesworth, *European Sculpture from Romanesque to Rodin* (Thames & Hudson), pp. 111–112.
274. The technique is further refined in the *Ascension* relief of c.1430 in the Victoria and Albert Museum, London.
275. See Bennett and Wilkins, op. cit. pp. 214–216.
276. Compiled about the year 1275. Though it does not appear to have been among the earliest printed books, the *Legenda Aurea* was no sooner in type than edition after edition appeared with surprising rapidity. It was certainly well known to Renaissance artists.
277. Op. cit. p. 217.
278. Rarely have the various attempts at dating the work diverged so considerably over many years of research. 1427 has been given as the earliest and 1460 as the latest date of creation. See Rolf C. Wirtz, *Donatello 1386–1466* (Könemann Verlaggesellschaft, Cologne, 1998), p. 69.
279. See note 164, op. cit. p. 218.
280. Bennett and Wilkins, op. cit., p. 218.
281. Ibid. p. 219.
282. Emil Bock, *Kings and Prophets* (Floris Books, 1989), p. 59.
283. We are reminded here of the *Gallant Tailor* by Jacob and Wilhelm Grimm.
284. The bronze relief panel is one of six surrounding the basin of the baptismal font in Siena cathedral.
285. See Molesworth, op. cit. p. 111.
286. Wölfflin op. cit. p. 6.
287. *The Renaissance in Florence* (George Weidenfeld & Nicholson Ltd., 1997), p. 95.
288. Ibid. p. 102.
289. Nesca Robb, *Neoplatonism of the Italian Renaissance*, p. 24.
290. See previous note, p. 33.
291. See note 110, ibid. p. 50.
292. Stefania Patinella, in her essay *From Plato to Neoplatonism. Love, Beauty, and women in the Symposium and Three Neoplatonic Texts.* Writes: 'Though Neoplatonism undoubtedly has Platonist philosophy at its core, it is not by any means a faithful or exact revival of Platonist doctrines. Rather, it is a mutation with both Christian ideals and the social conventions of Renaissance Italy as its transforming agents'.

    See also: http://ccat.sas.upenn.edu/italians/resources/amiciprize/1997.
293. See F.W. Zeylmans van Emmichoven, *The Reality in Which We Live* (New Knowledge Books, 1964), ch. VIII.